Wolfstein Sculpture Parks

At Scripps Memorial Hospitals San Diego

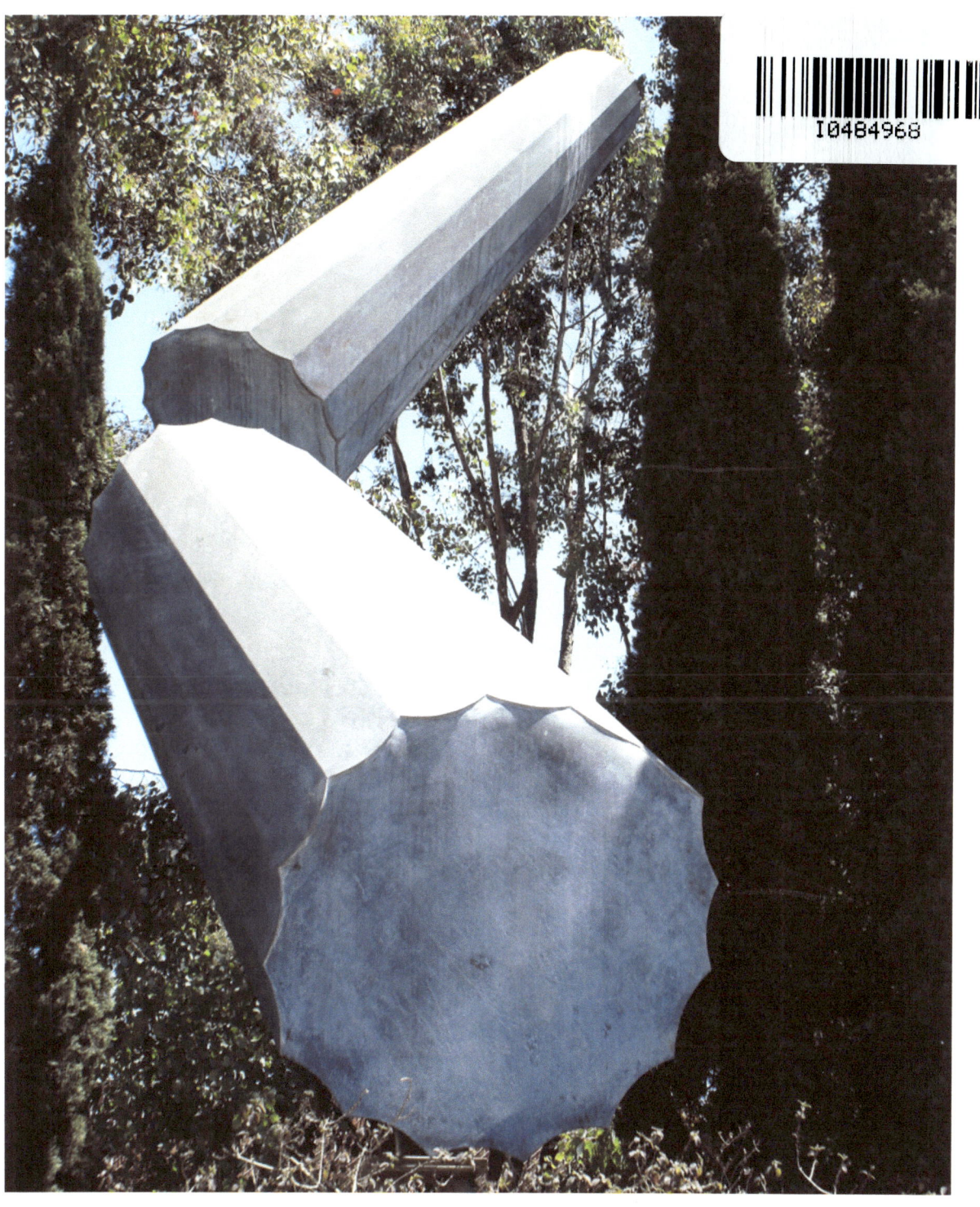

By Gerrit Greve

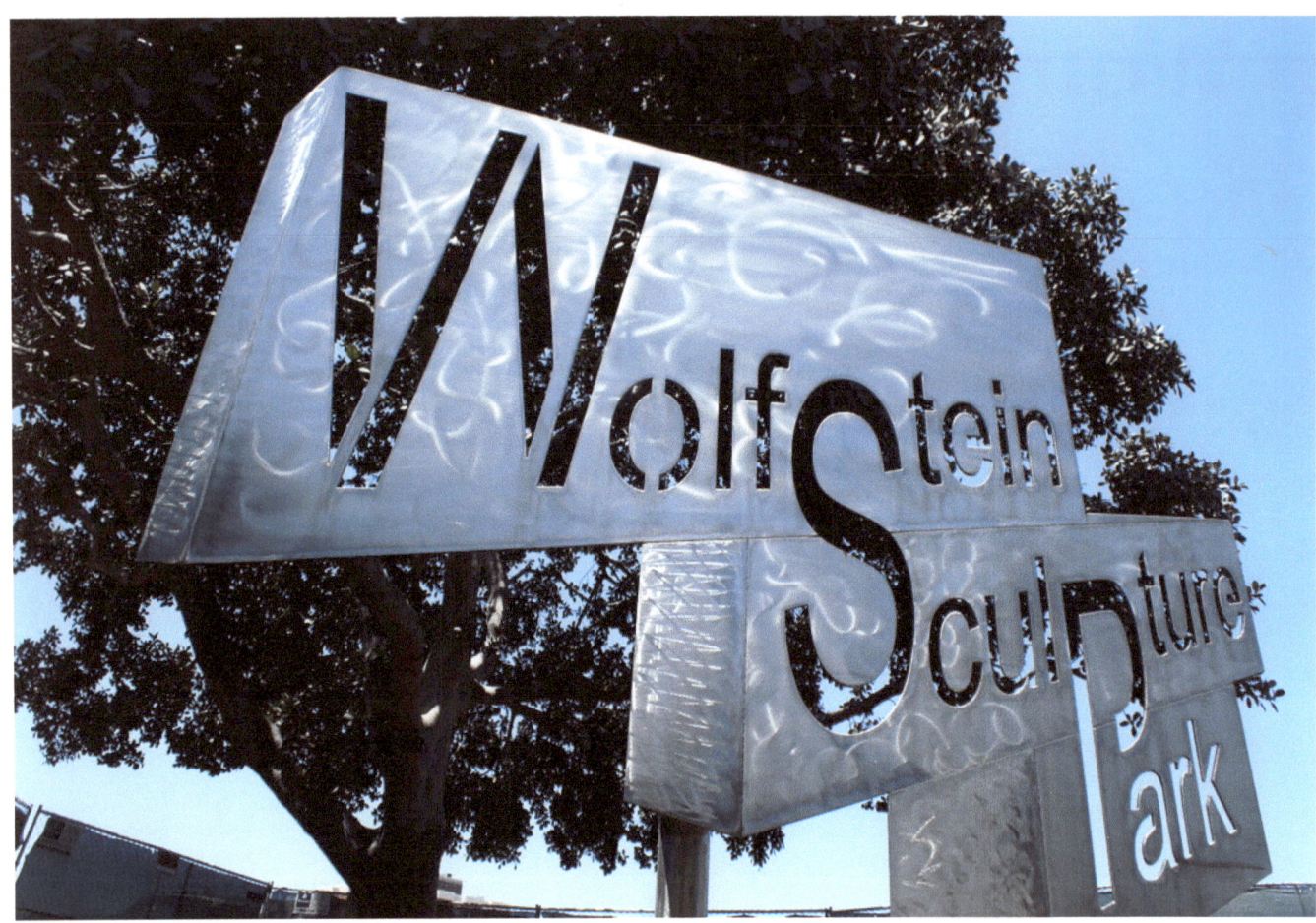

The impact of the arts in the process of healing was recognized early on by Hippocrates, who understood the importance of uplifting his patients' spirits. Similarly, Galen would set his patients outside in the marketplace, enhancing their healing through contact with the sights and sounds of daily life. The value of a rich and uplifting environment to healing has since been documented in recent research which has demonstrated that patients who could view nature through their windows had shorter post-operative hospital stays, made negative comments less often, needed fewer doses of narcotics, and had fewer post-surgical complications.

In recent years, there has been a dramatic growth in the use of the arts in medicine - thanks to the pioneering work of Hospital Audiences, Inc., the Duke University Medical Center, the Planetree Hospitals, and the Society for the Arts in Healthcare, amongst others, as well as the work by such visionaries as the Wolfsteins. This growth has taken place in numerous hospitals, hospices, medical schools, and other centers of healing.

For Further Information: **wolfsteinsculptureparks.com**

Photography by: Sue and Clint Degn, Ralyn Wolfstein, and Gerrit Greve.

Edited by: Ralyn Wolfstein, and Gerrit Greve.

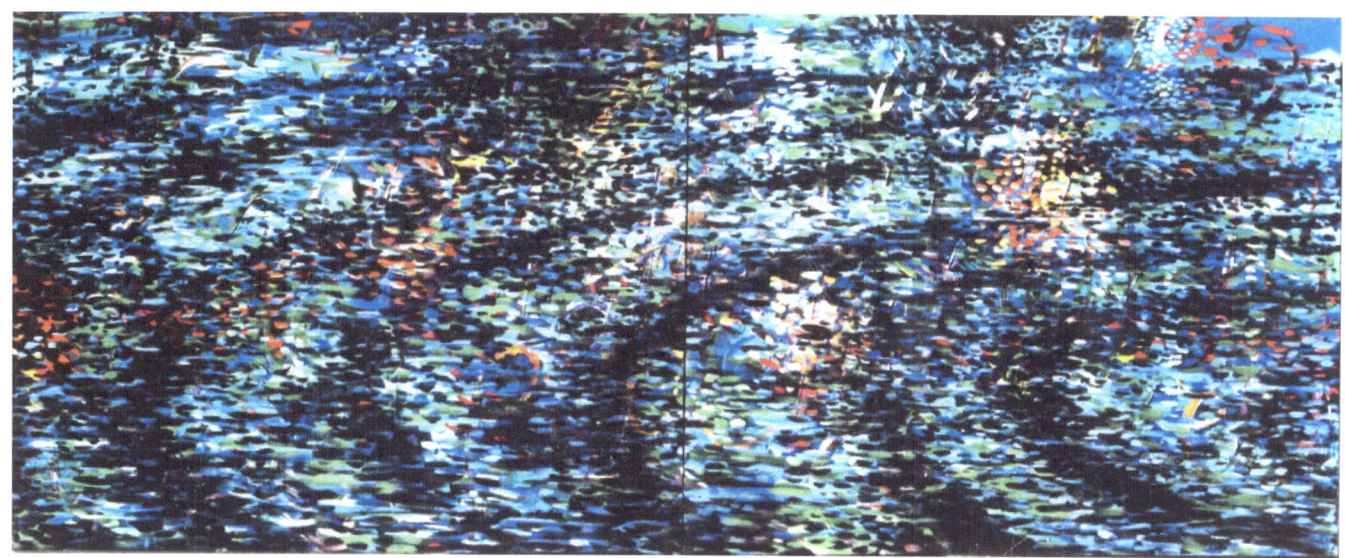

"Truth Lies Just Beneath the Surface" by Gerrit Greve

In 1993, in honor of their 45th wedding anniversary, Ralyn and Nathan Wolfstein presented this Gerrit Greve painting, in order to bring their Arts for Healing program to Scripps. This painting is still enjoyed today by visitors who pass through the main lobby of Scripps Memorial Hospital La Jolla, California. This visionary program had originated with the Wolfsteins at the University of California Irvine - Cancer Center in 1991.

To celebrate their 50th wedding anniversary in 1998, the Wolfsteins made a gift to establish the Wolfstein Sculpture Park. The vision was to enhance the course of healing for patients, their families, visitors, and staff, by integrating art with a healing environment. The Wolfsteins were so moved by the beauty of the surrounding grounds of the hospital, that they also donated five sculptures that year to begin the sculpture park, a tradition they have continued and encouraged others to join.

Unless otherwise noted, all the sculptures in this book were donated by Ralyn and Nathan Wolfstein

Scripps Memorial Hospital La Jolla

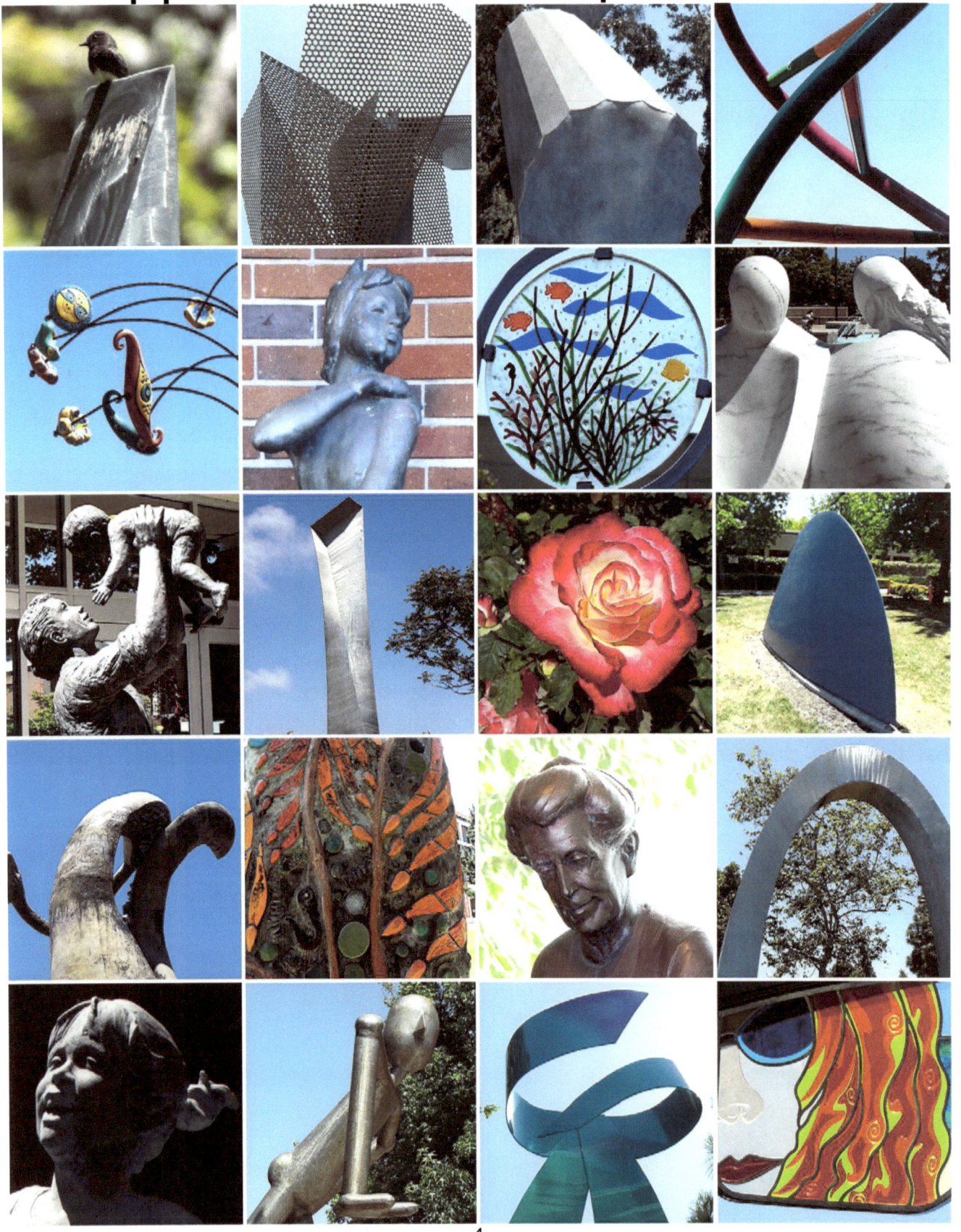

Scripps Memorial Hospital La Jolla

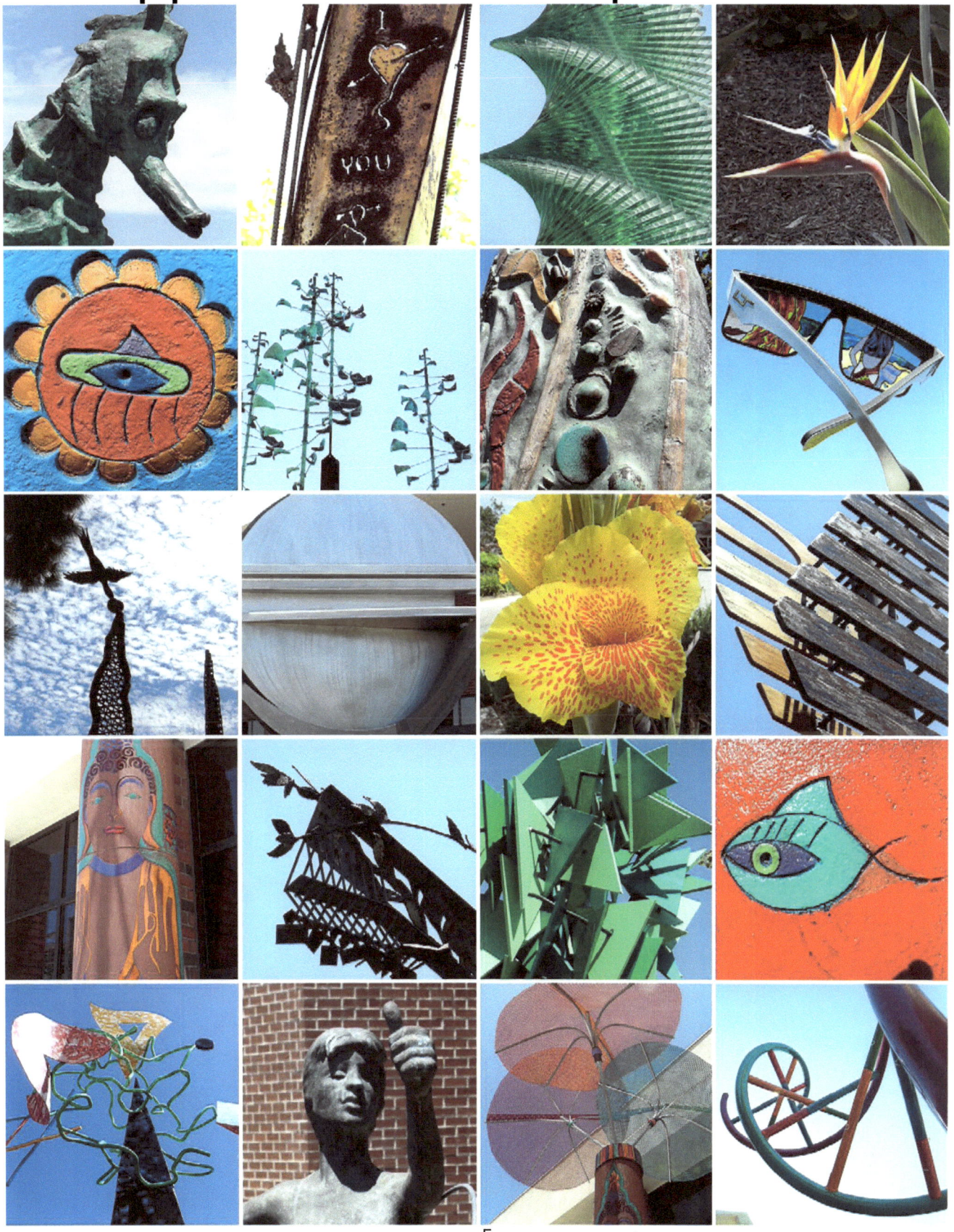

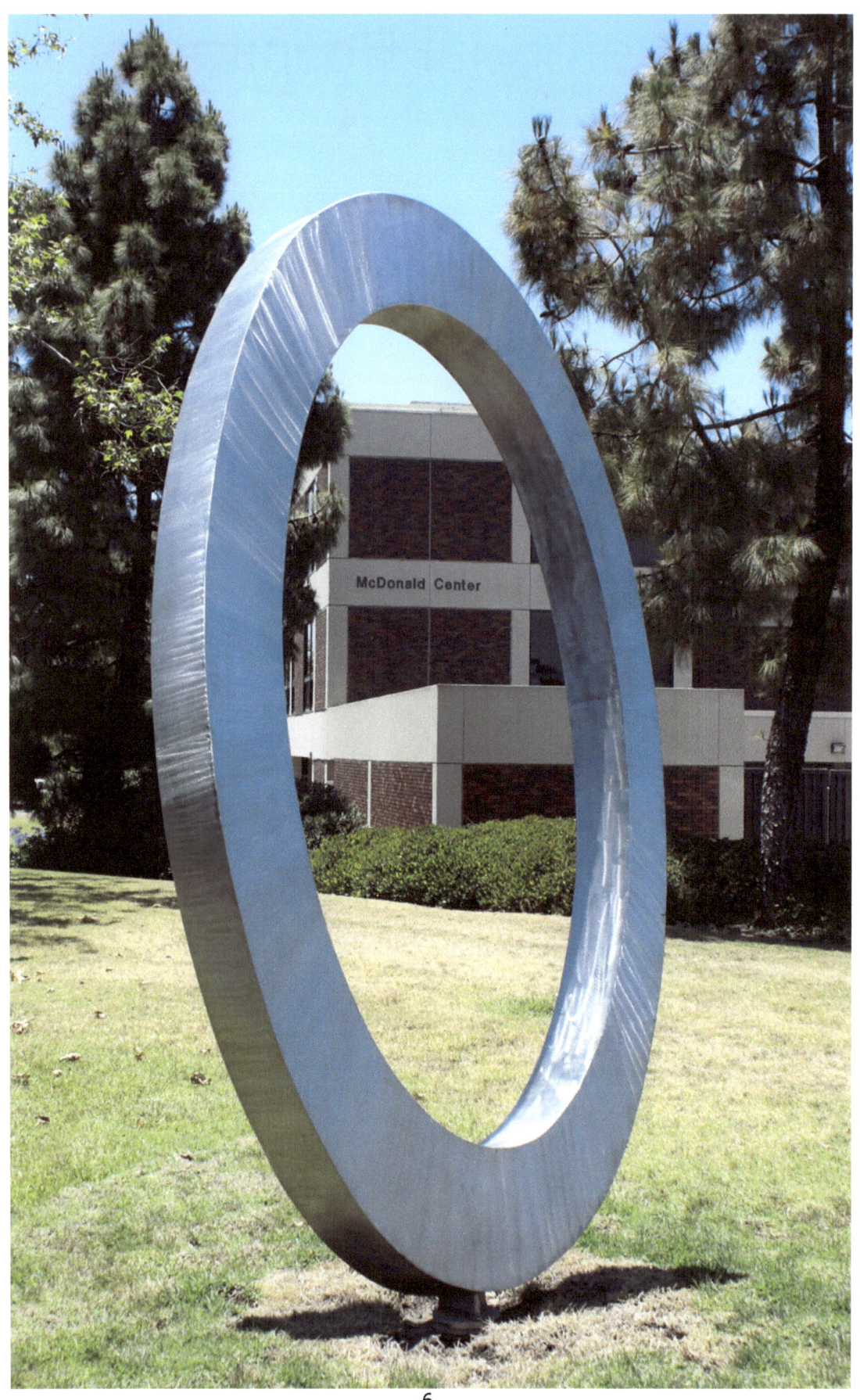

6

ONEIROMANCY by Jeffery Laudenslager

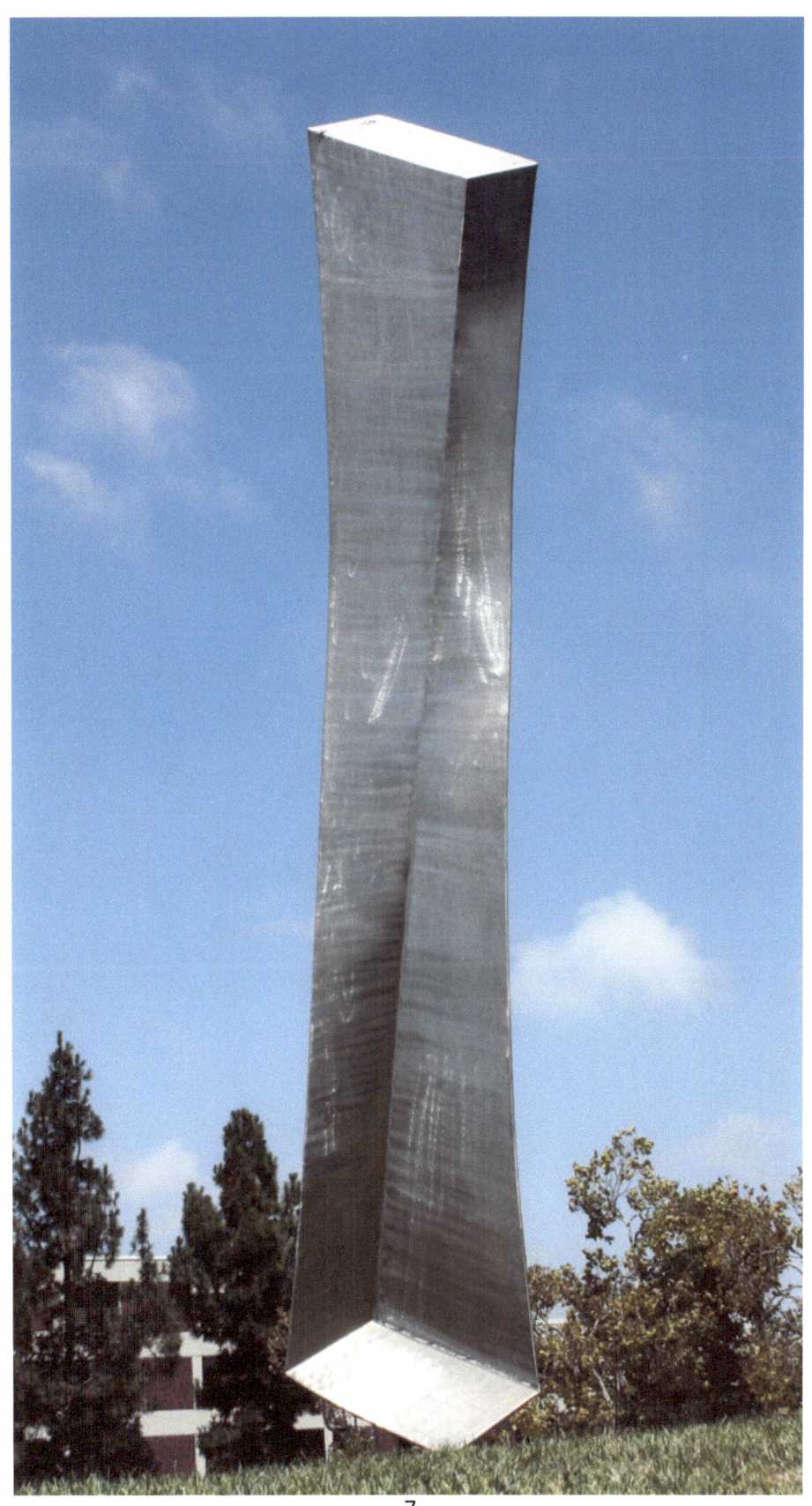

7

OBELUS by Jeffery Laudenslager

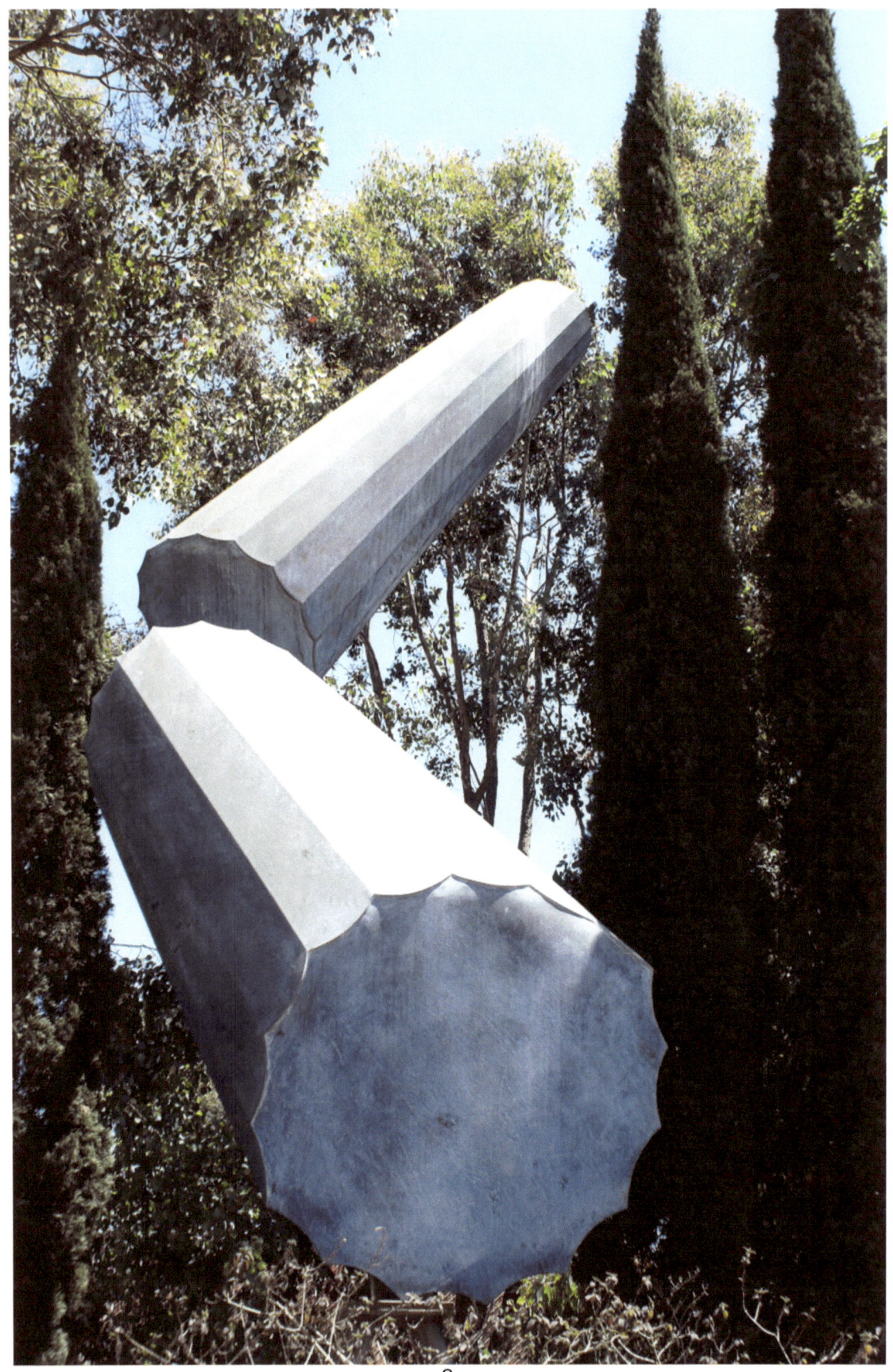

8

BRUTAL DANCE by Jeffery Laudenslager

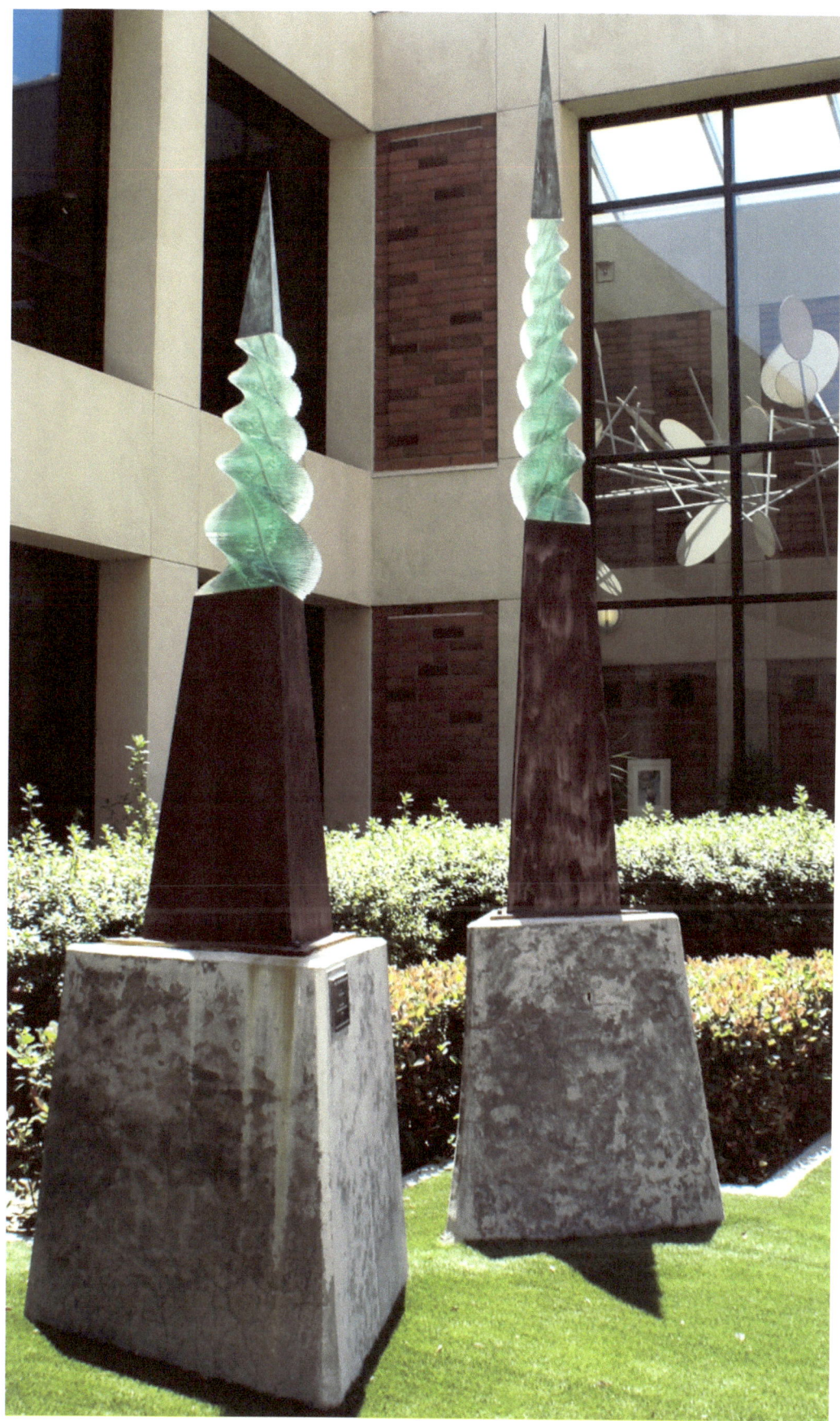

9

SPIRAL TETRAHEDRON 1 & 2 by Christopher Lee

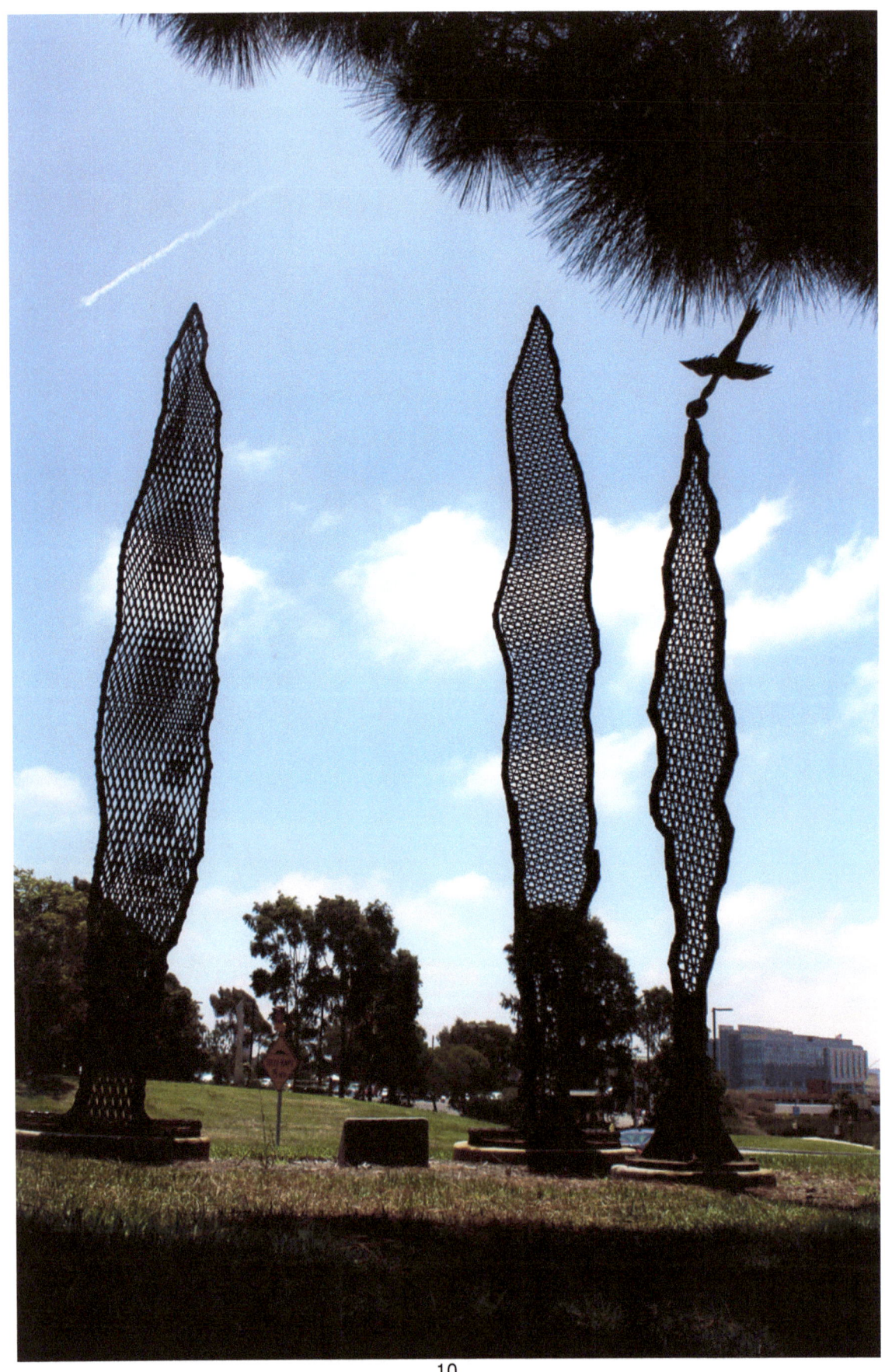

10
SYMBOLIC FOREST WITH ELIJA by Italo Scanga

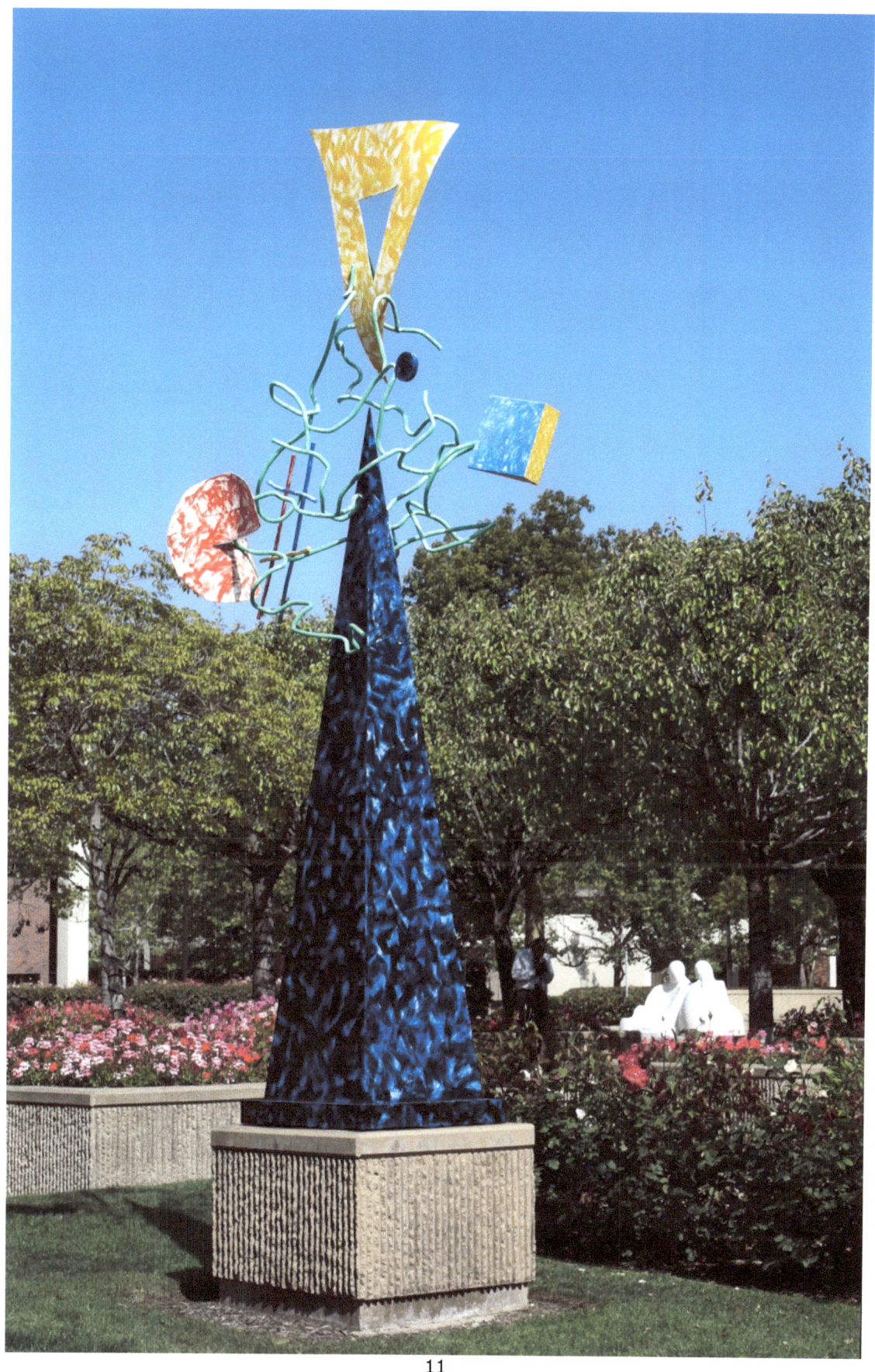

11
SCRIBBLE MOUNTAIN by Ron Tatro

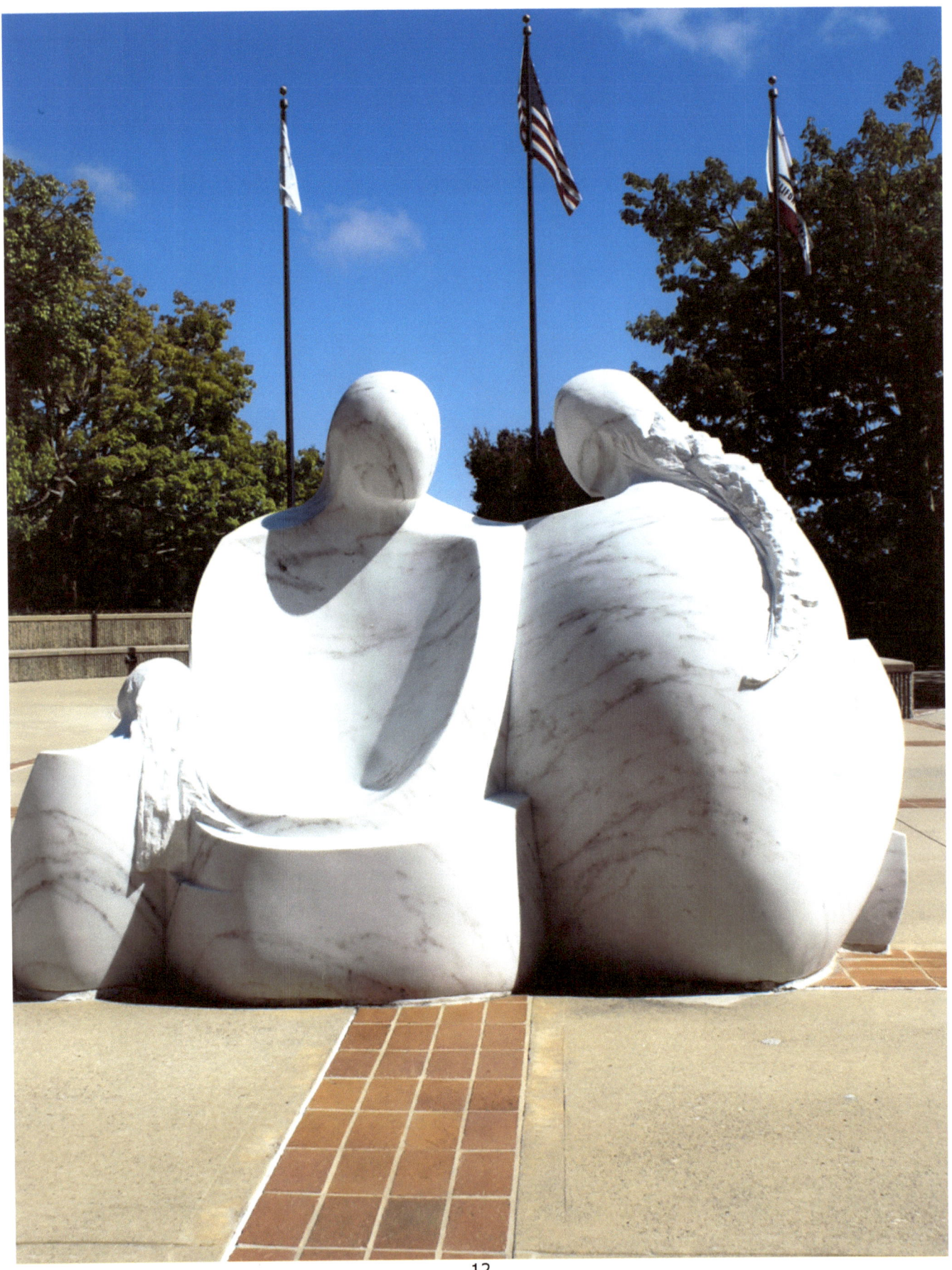

12

FAMILY REFLECTIONS by Madeline Wiener

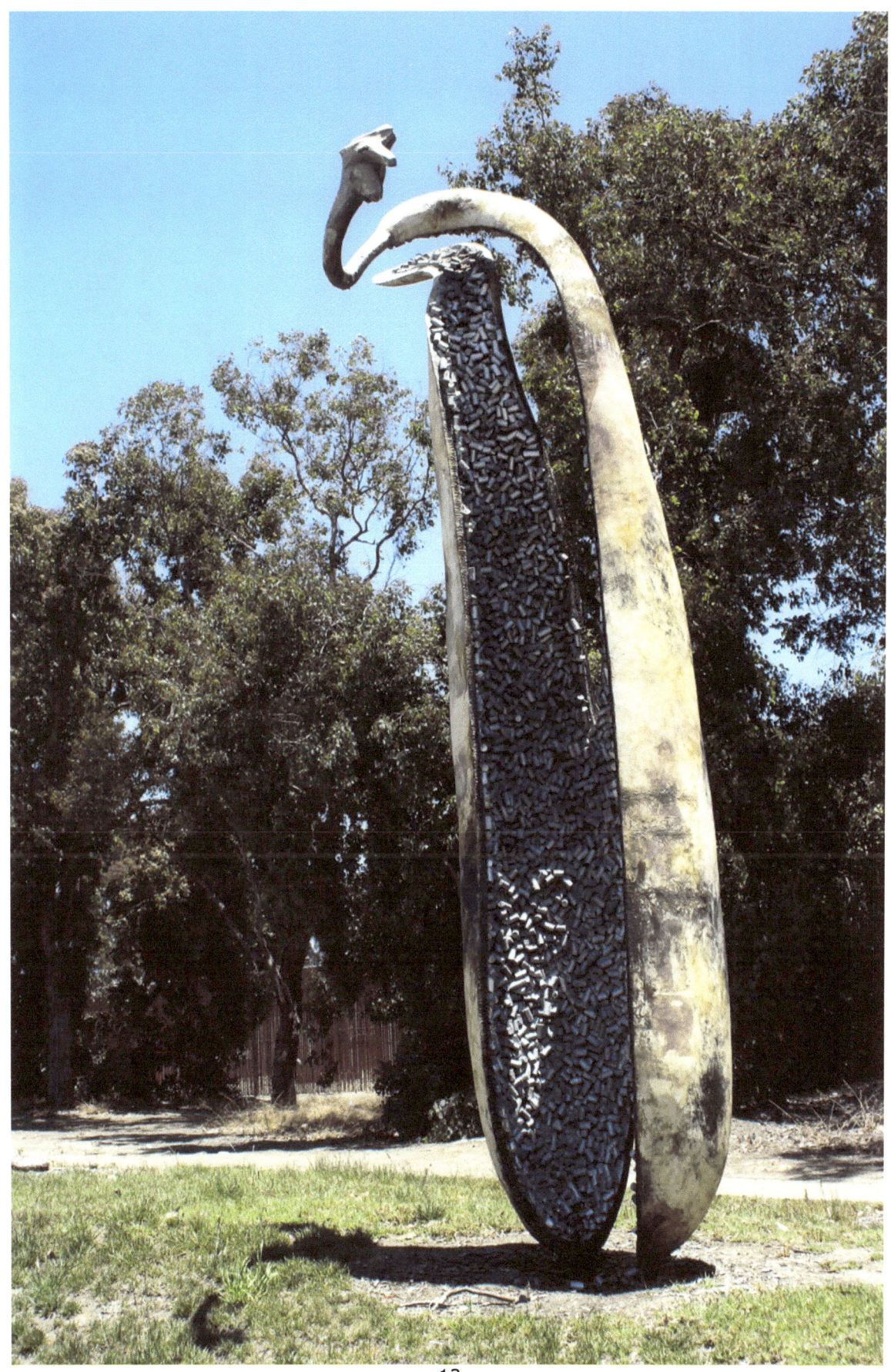

GODDESS GOURD by Becky Gutin

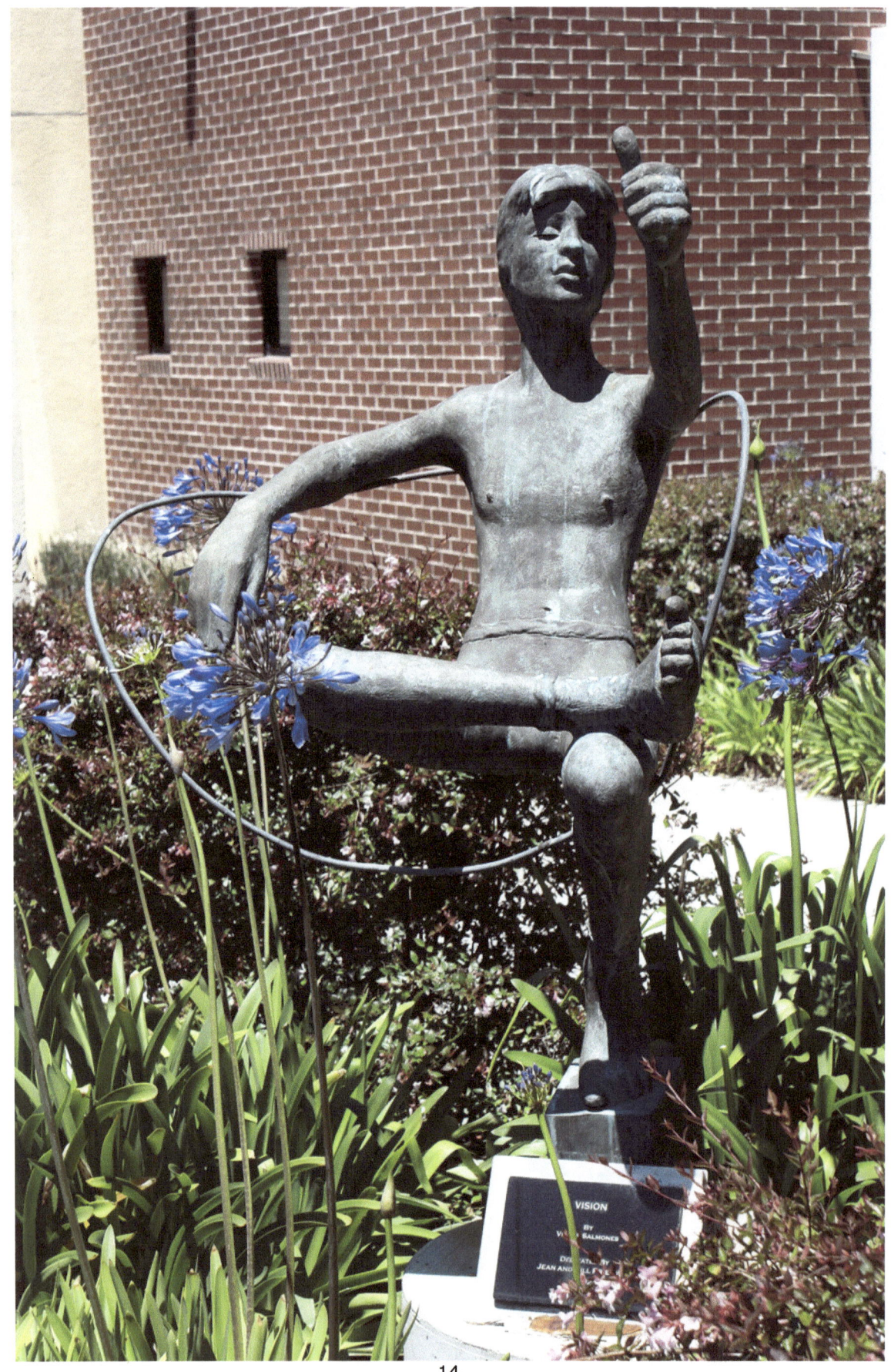

14

VISION by Victor Salmones [donated by Jean & William Friedman]

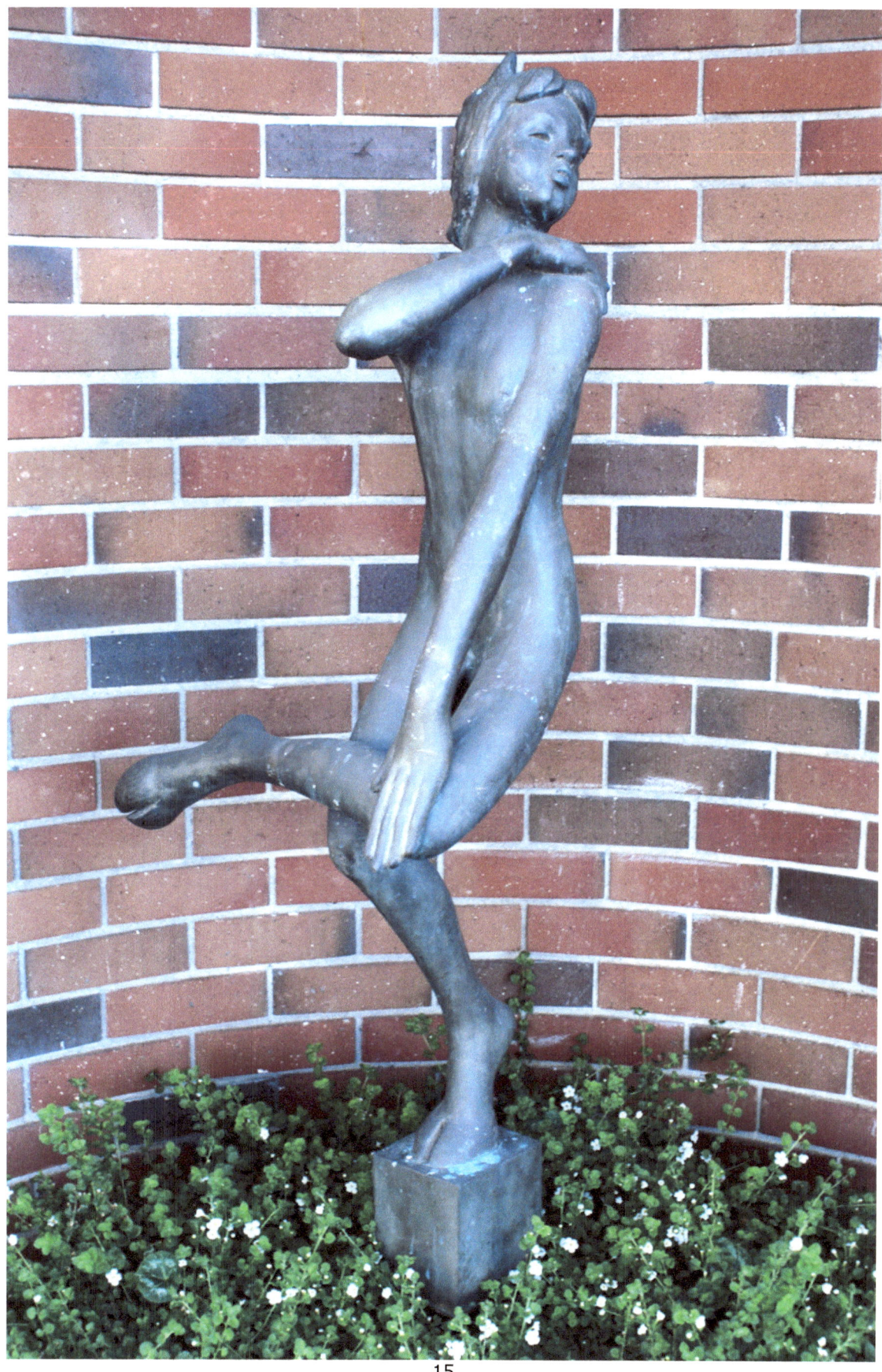

15

FANTASY by Victor Salmones [donated by Jean & William Friedman]

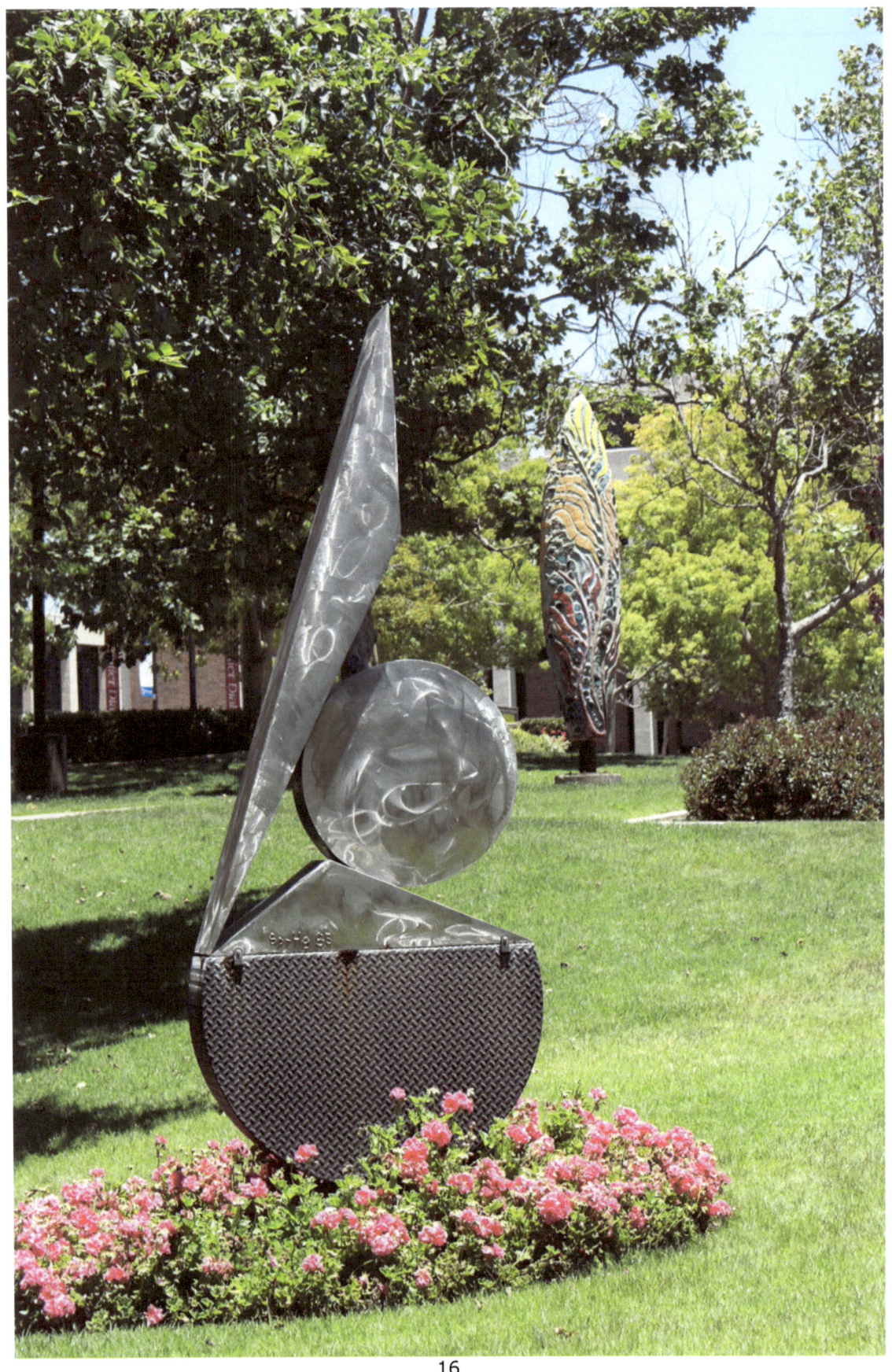

16
A NEW NOTE by Unknown Artist
[donated by Arden Realty, Jeffery Laudenslager, and the Wolfsteins]

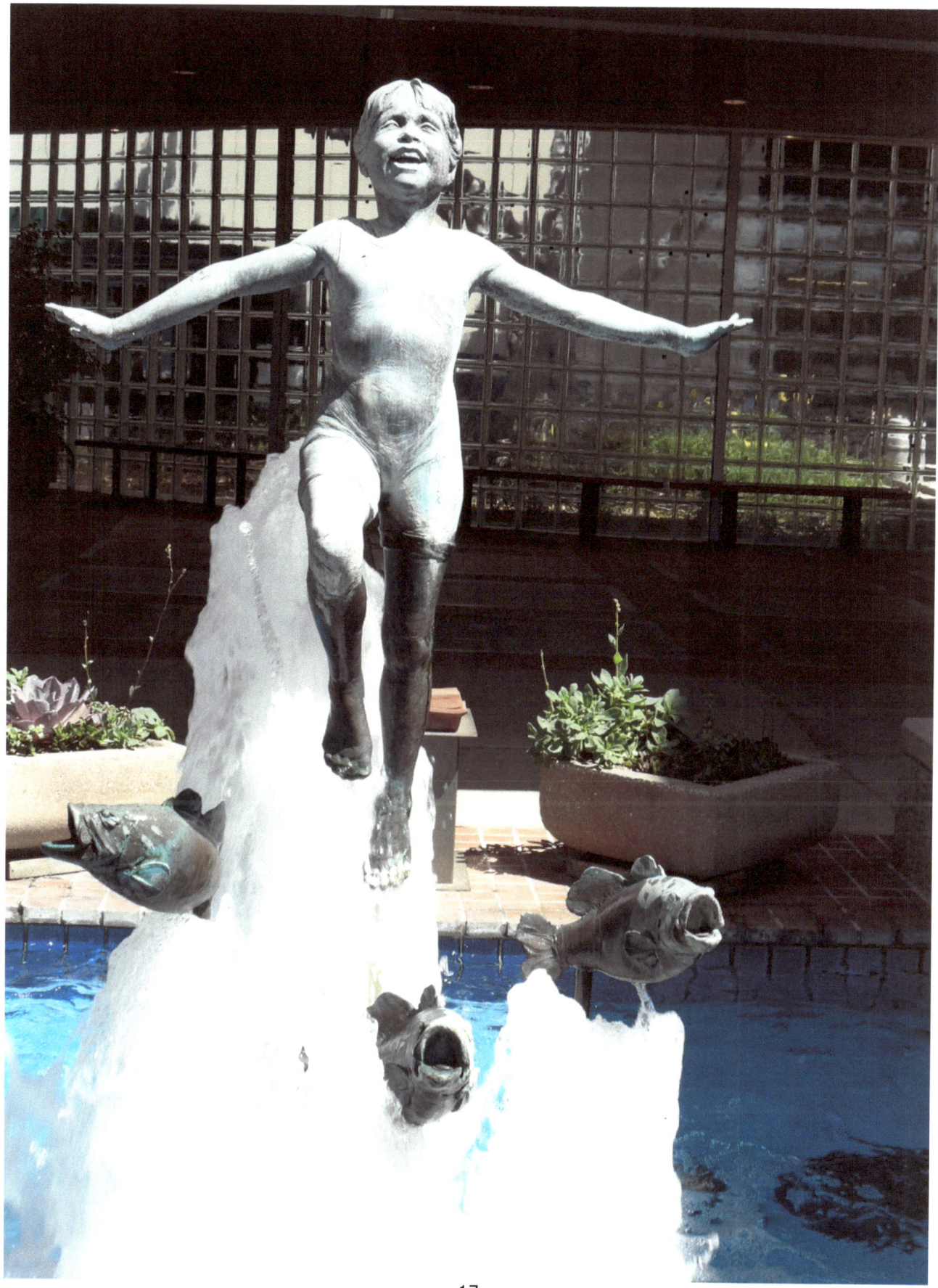

A LITTLE GIRL WITH FISHES by TJ Dixon & James Nelson

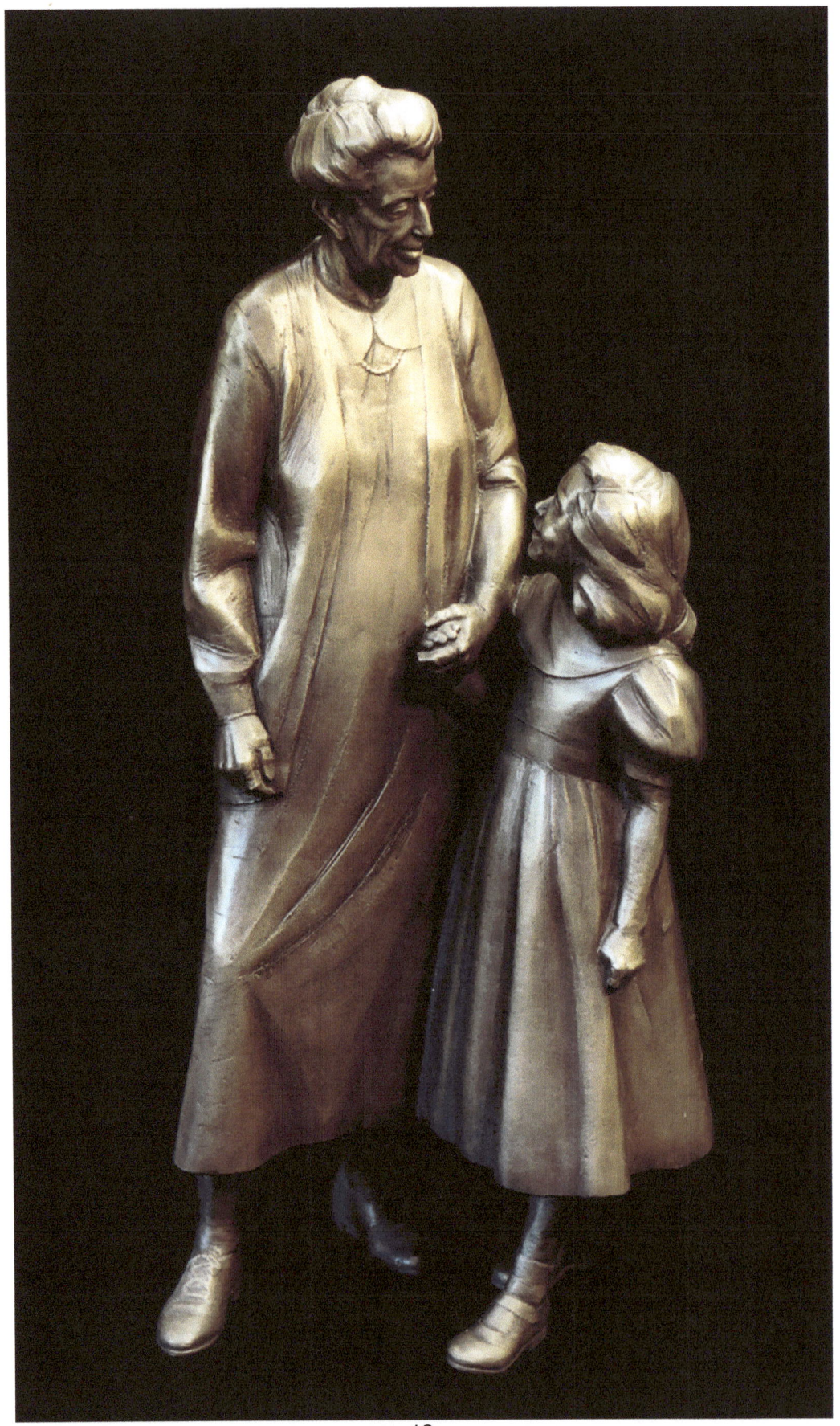

18
ELLEN BROWNING SCRIPPS by TJ Dixon & James Nelson [donated by Scripps Foundation]

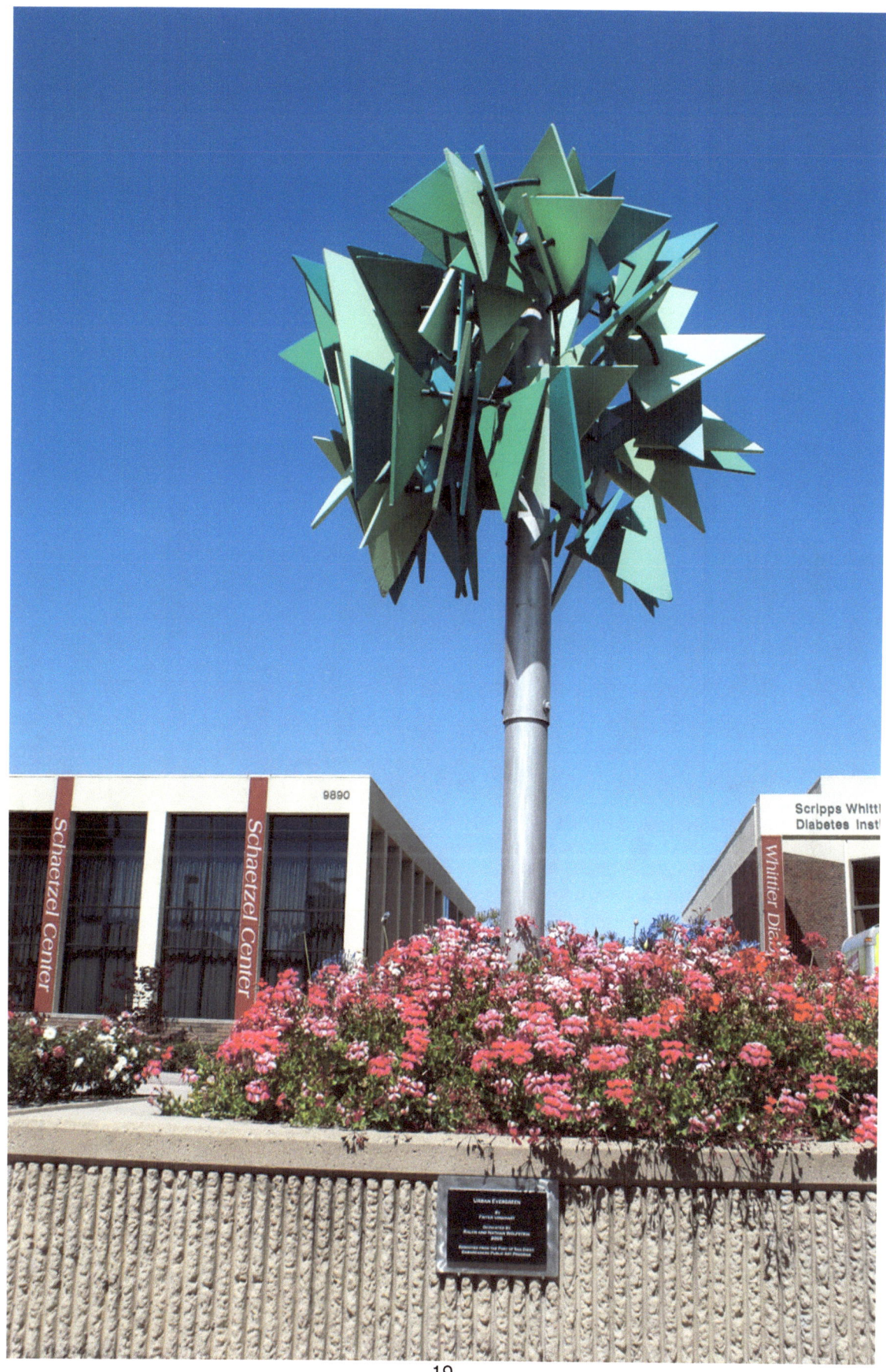

19

URBAN EVERGREEN by Fritzie Urquhart

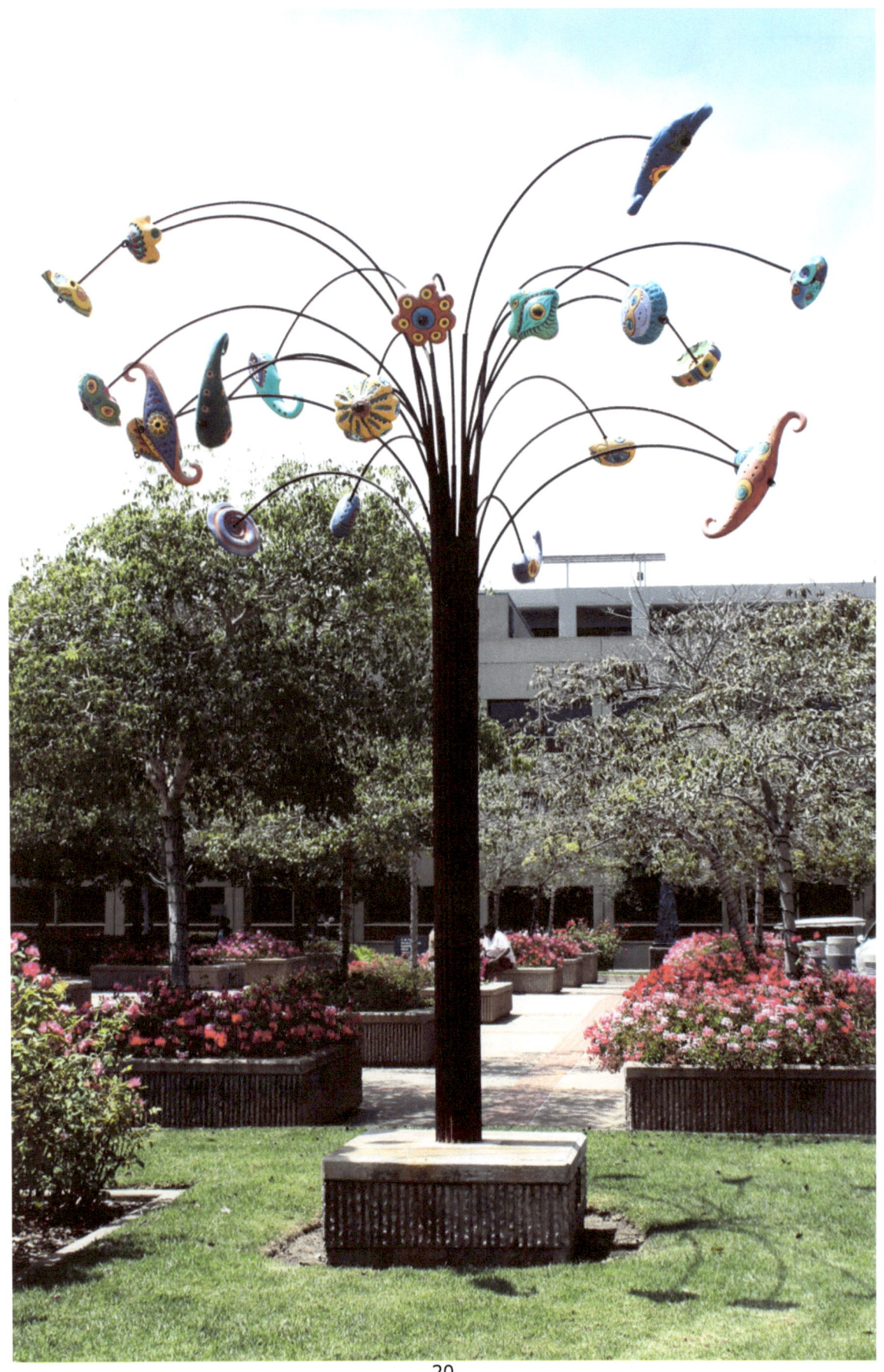

THE HAPPY TREE by Doug Snider & Linda Joanou

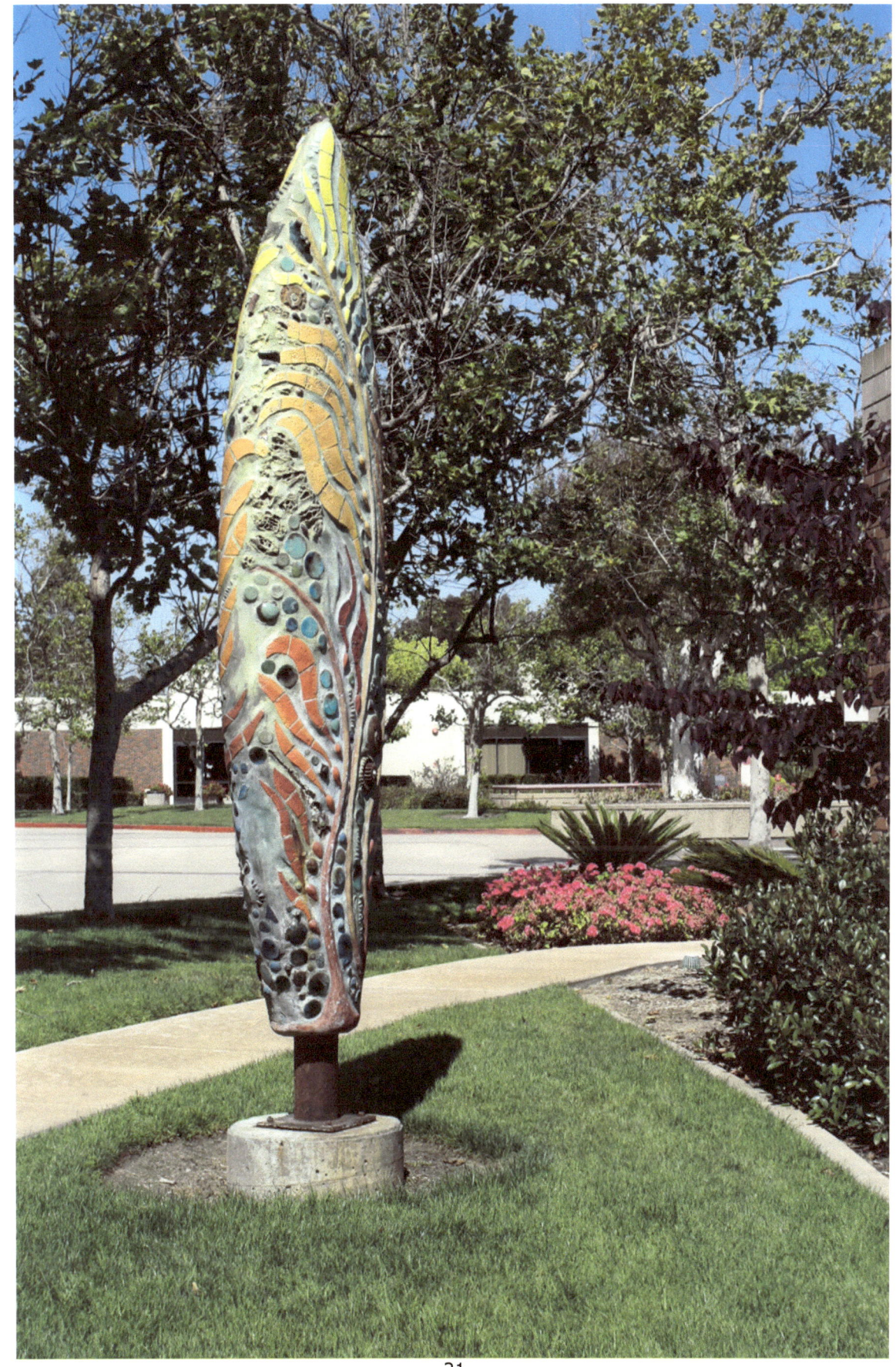

21
SURFBOARD CEDAR SURVIVOR by Betsy Kopshina Shulz & Hans Togebo

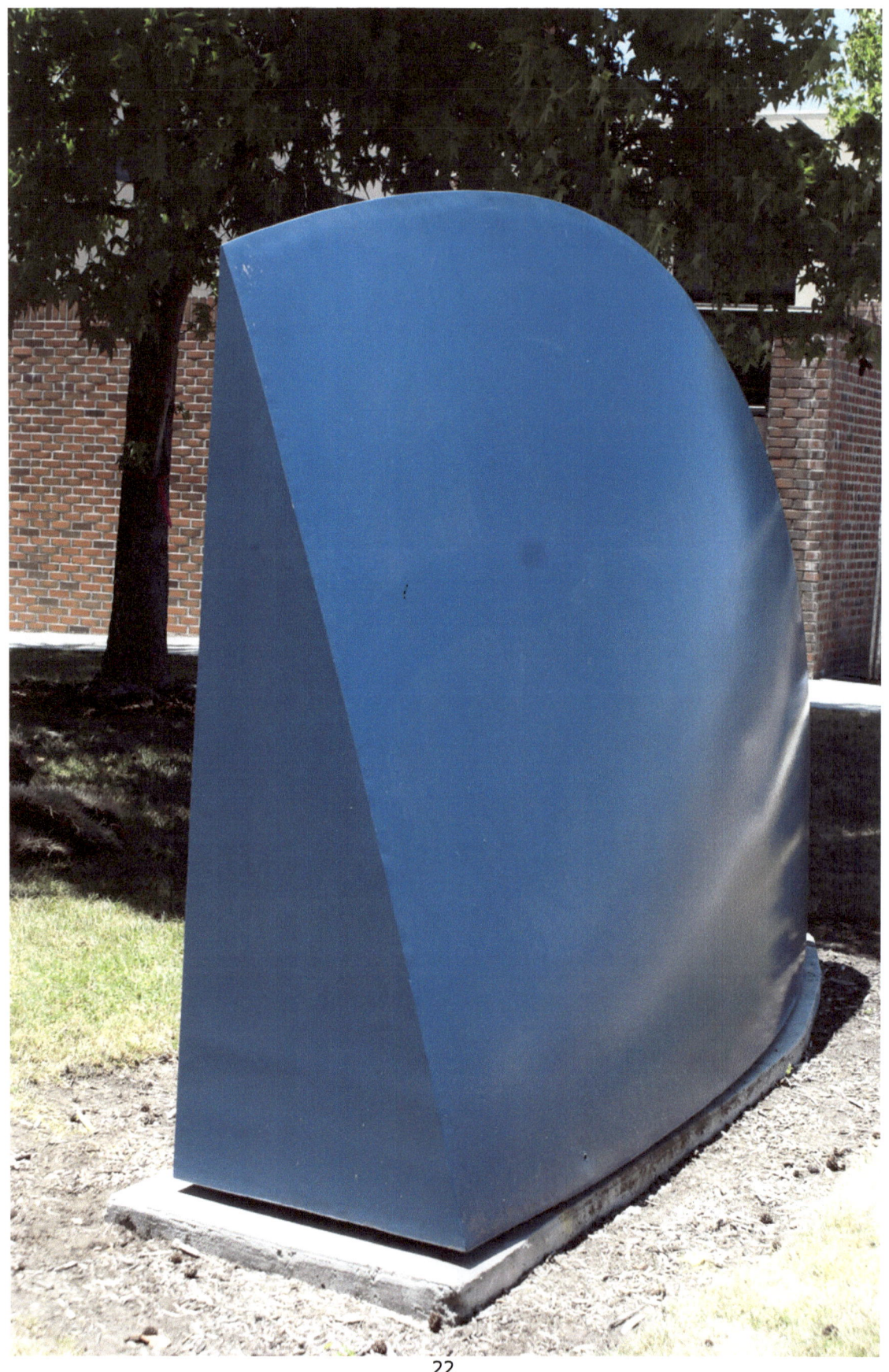

22
CORNER by Tom Waldren
[donated by Caroline & Charles Wegner, Jeffery Laudenslager, and the Wolfsteins]

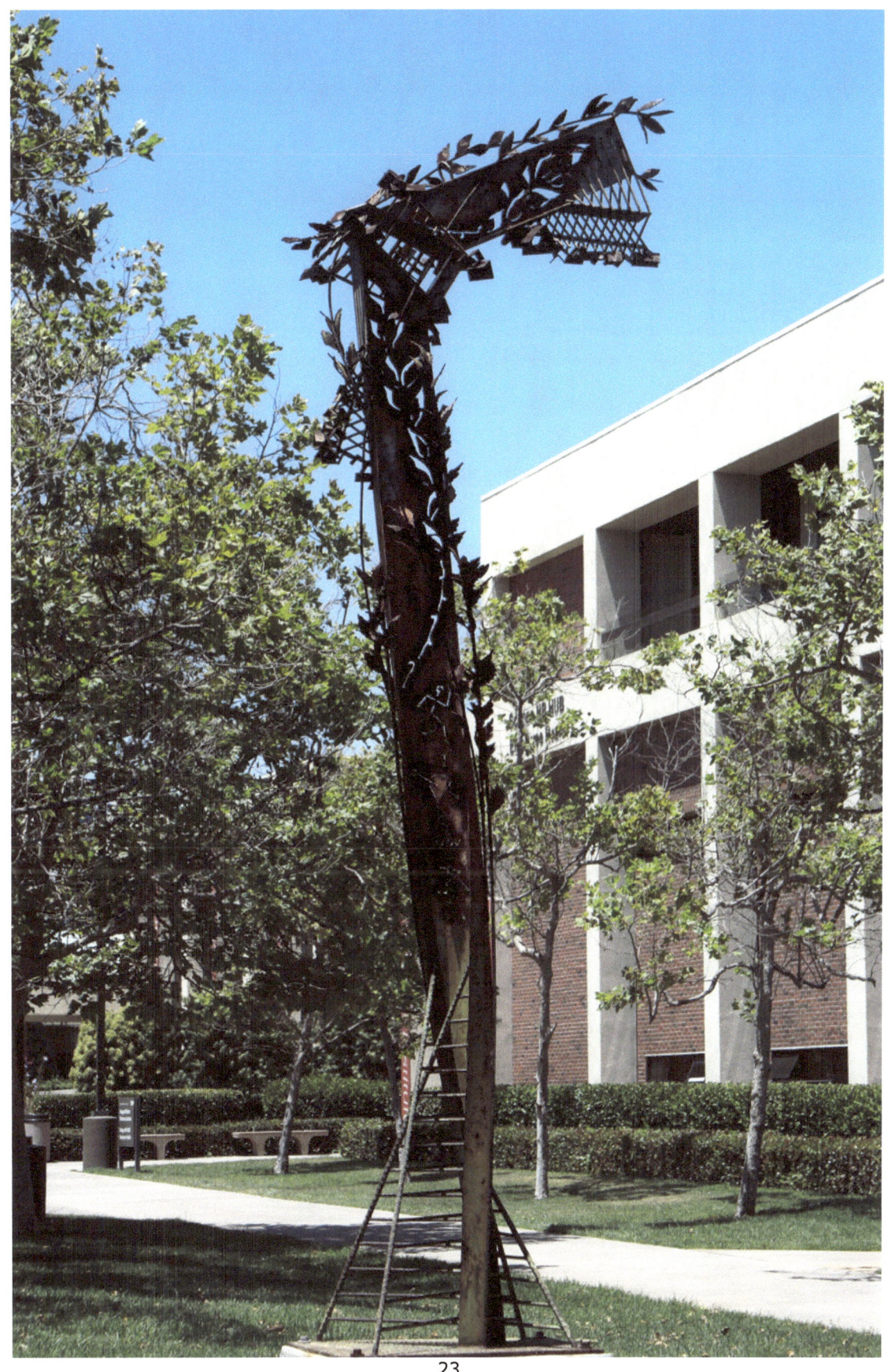

23
TREEHOUSE by Nasser Pirasteh
[donated by Scripps Memorial Hospital Radiology Department]

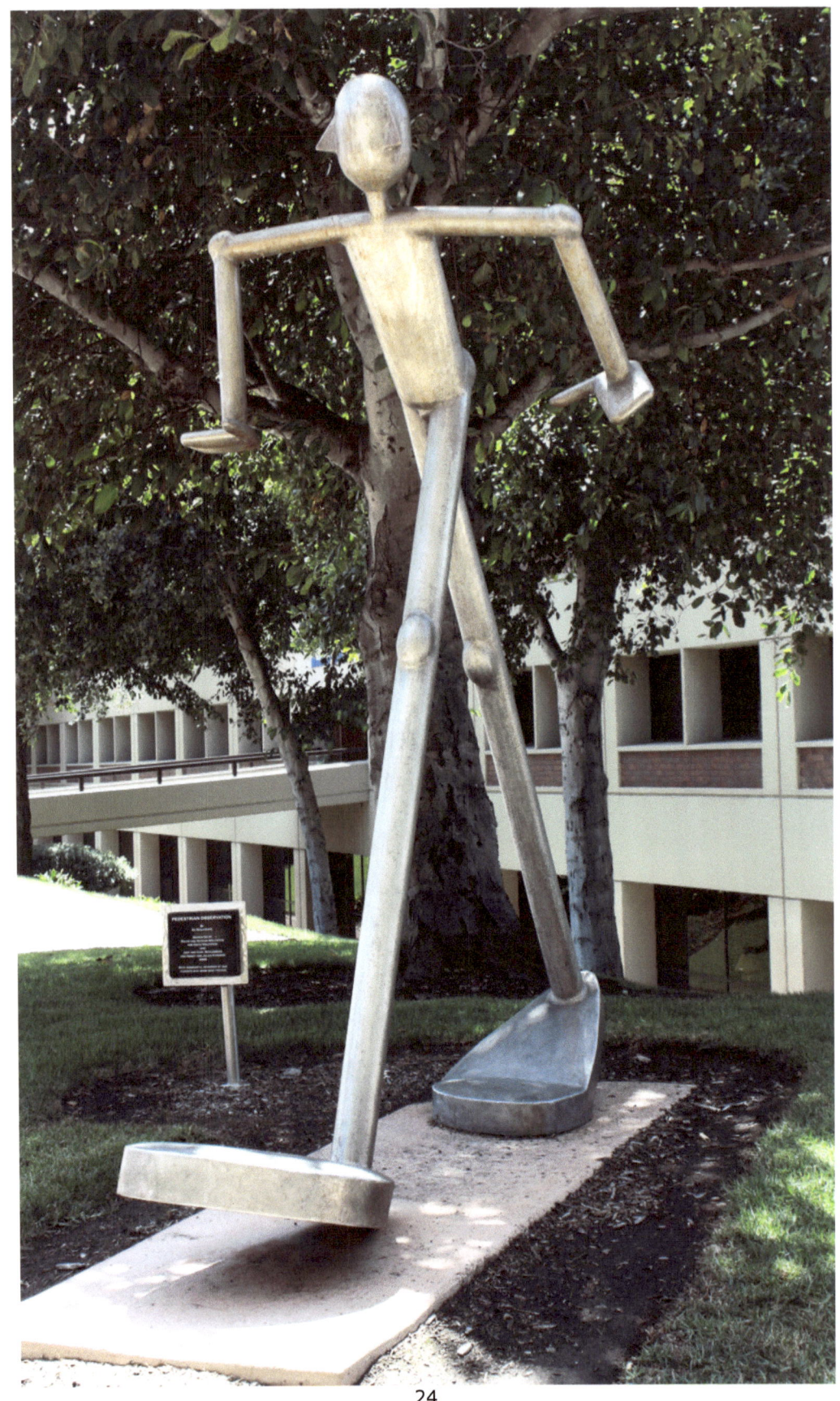

24
PEDESTRIAN OBSERVATION by Ed Benavente
[Donated by Ralyn & Nathan Wolfstein and Judy & Carl Schlosberg]

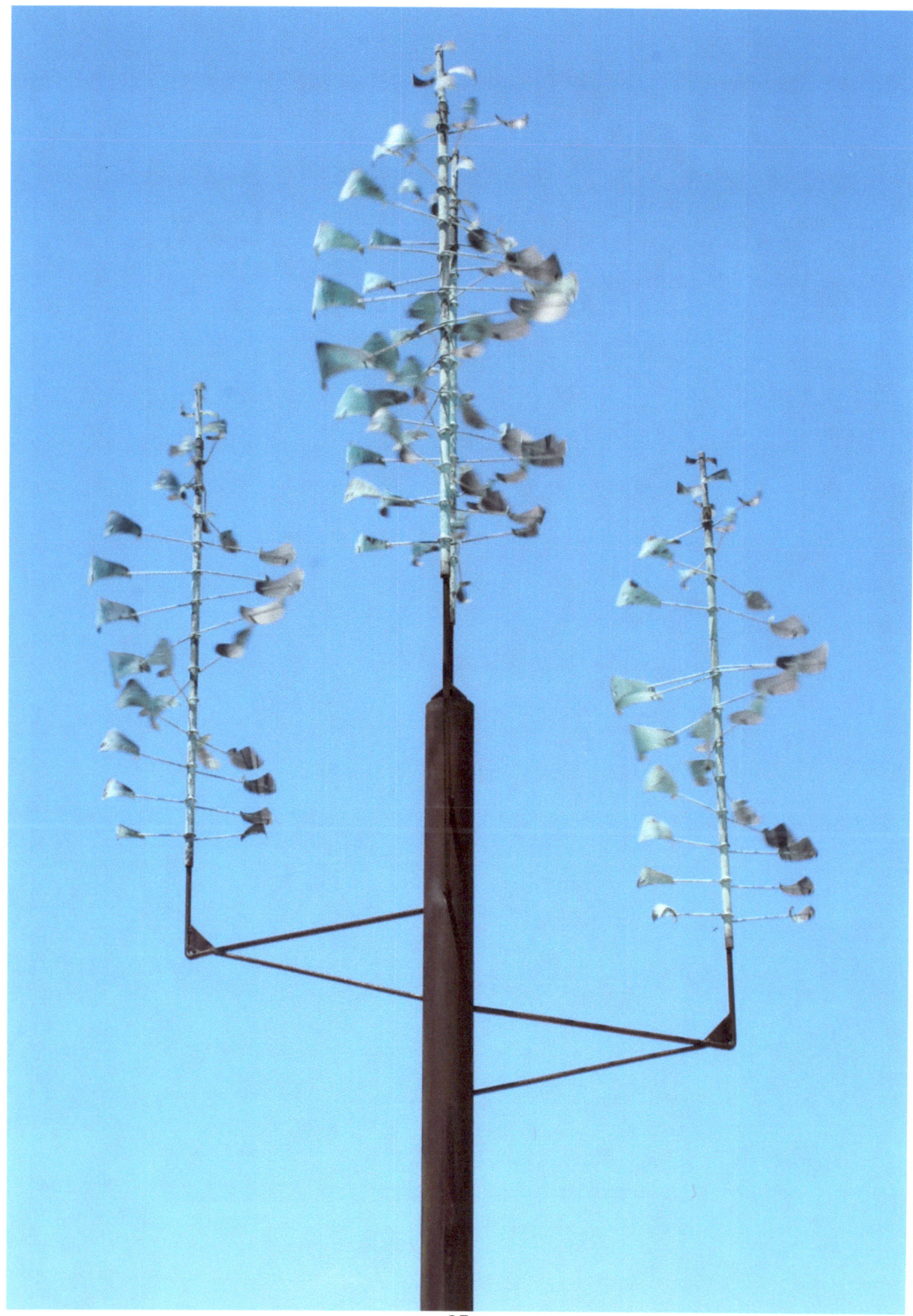

25
WINDANCER by Amos Robinson & Ken Chytraus

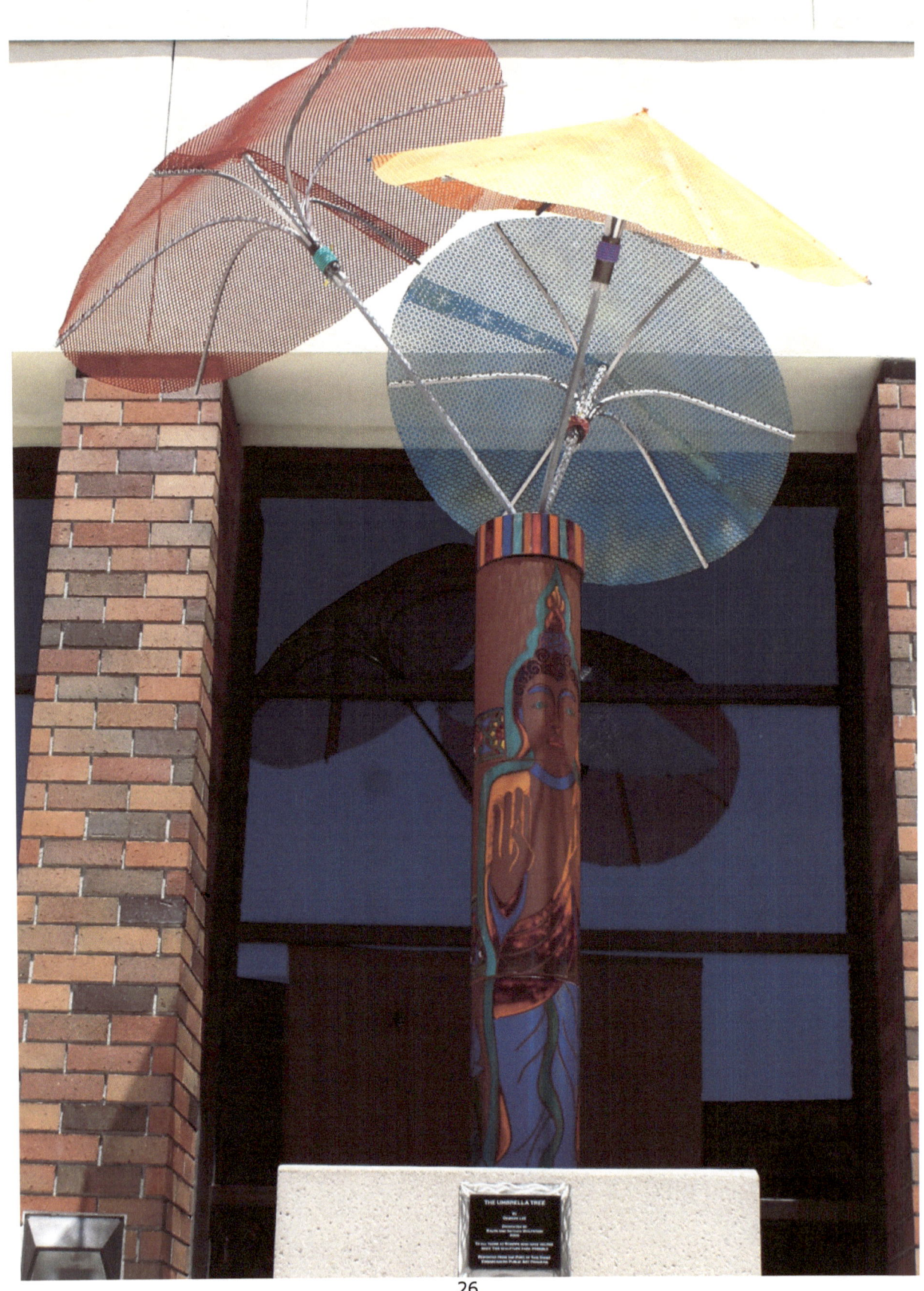

THE UMBRELLA TREE by Deirdre Lee

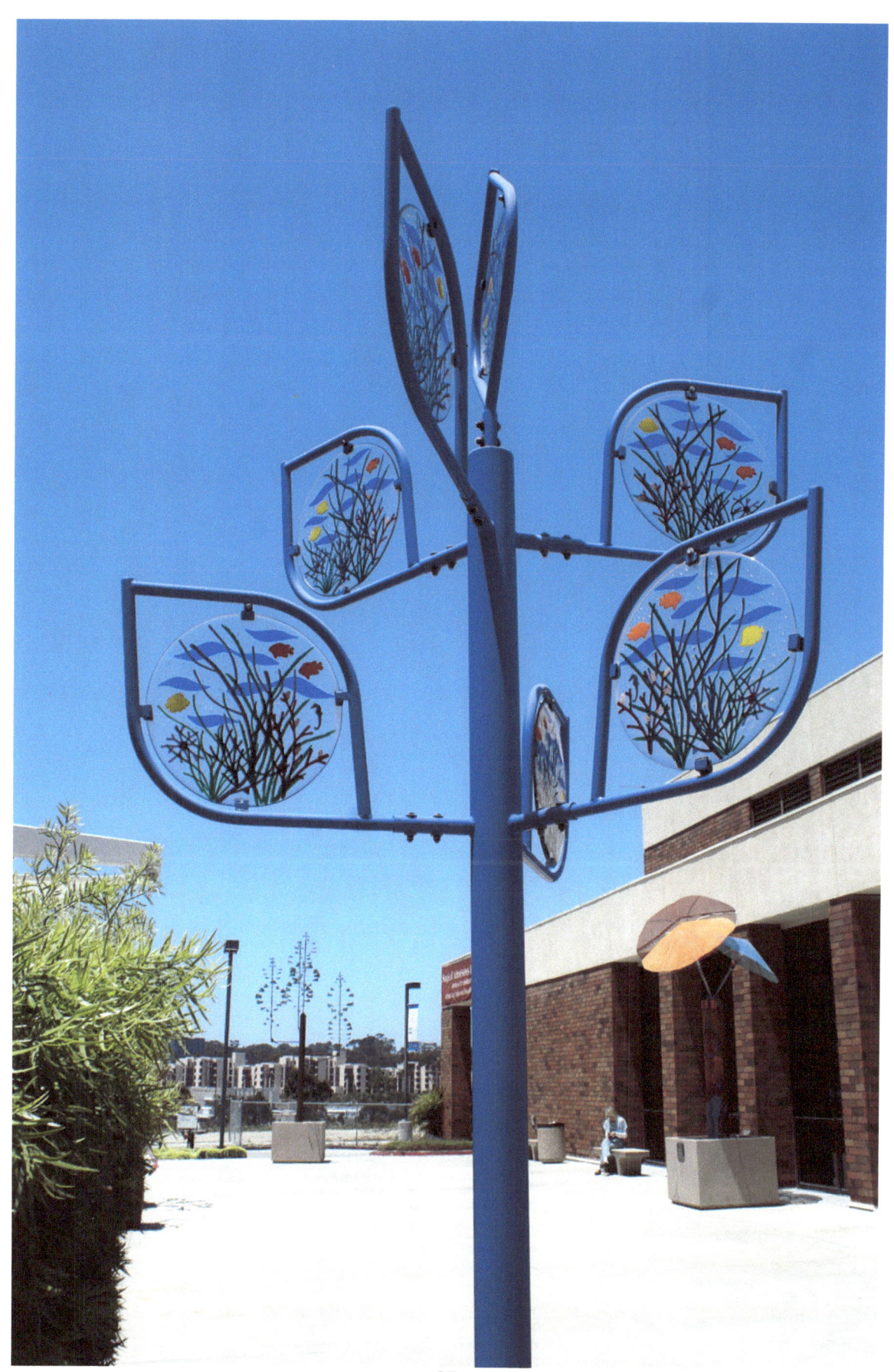

27
CNIDARIAN DREAMS by Bobby Valdez

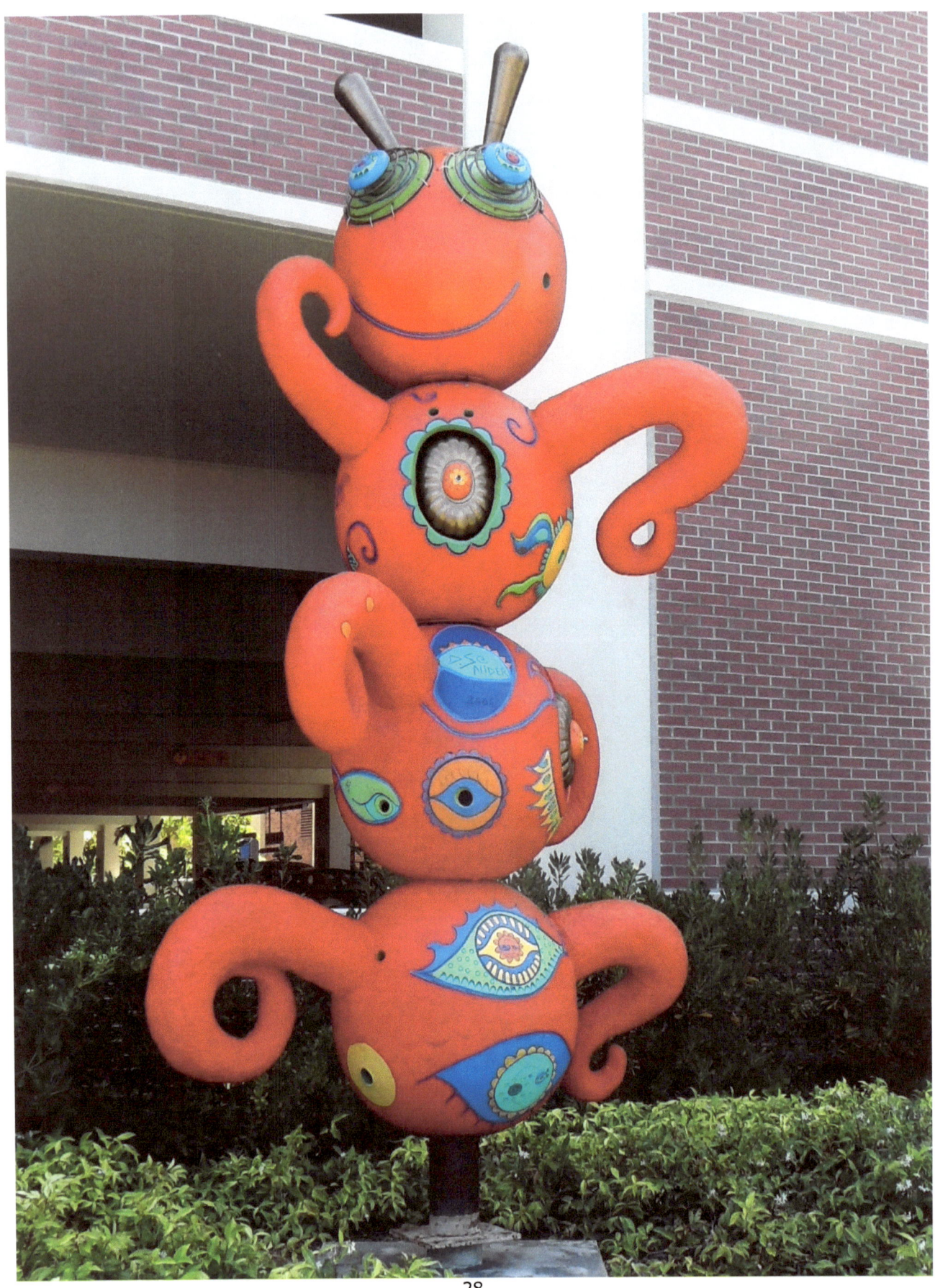

28
TANGERINE CATERPILLAR DREAM by Doug Snider & Sara Storm

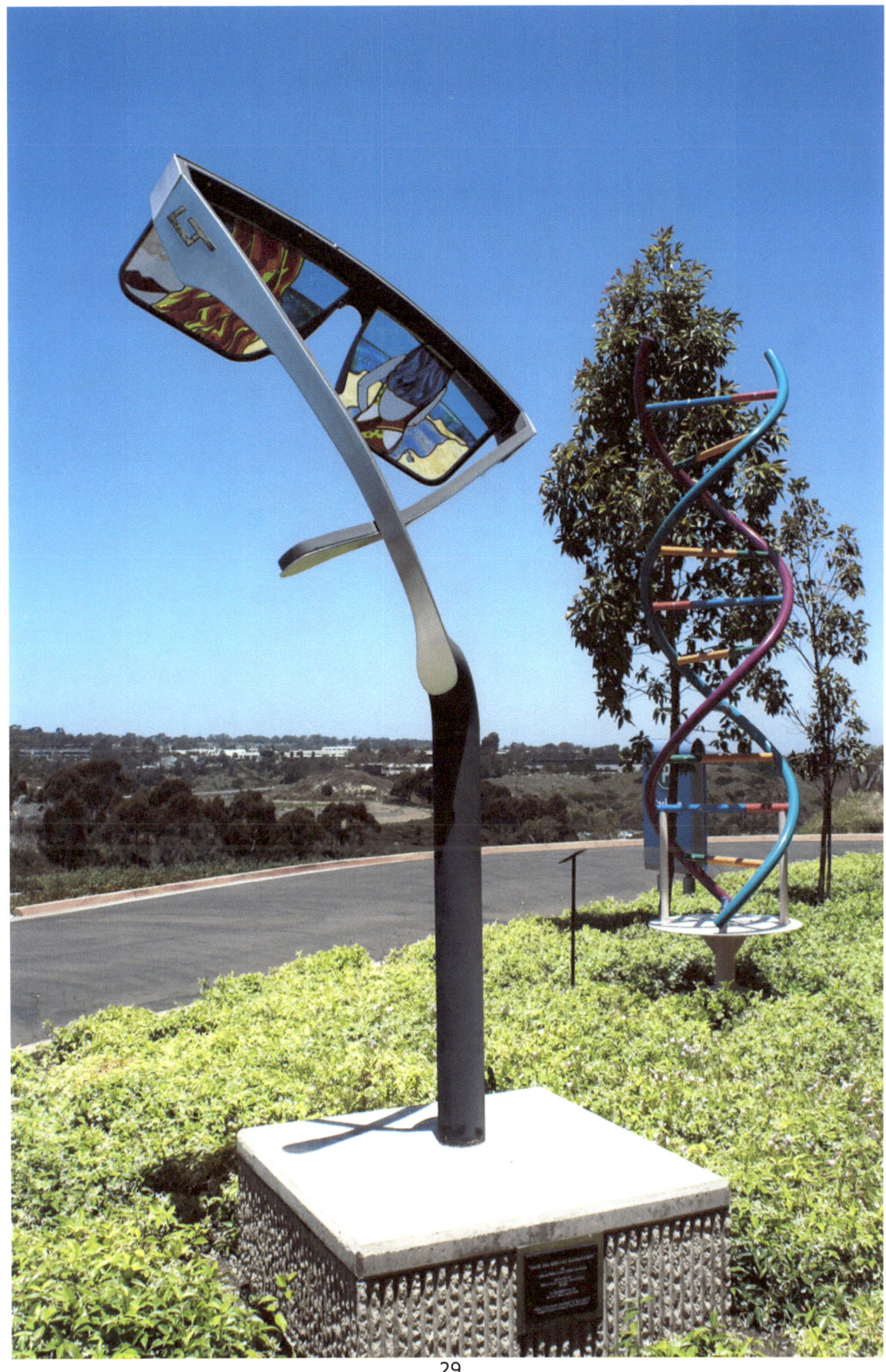

HAVE YOU SEEN MY SUNGLASSES by Leslie Perlis & Terry Douglas

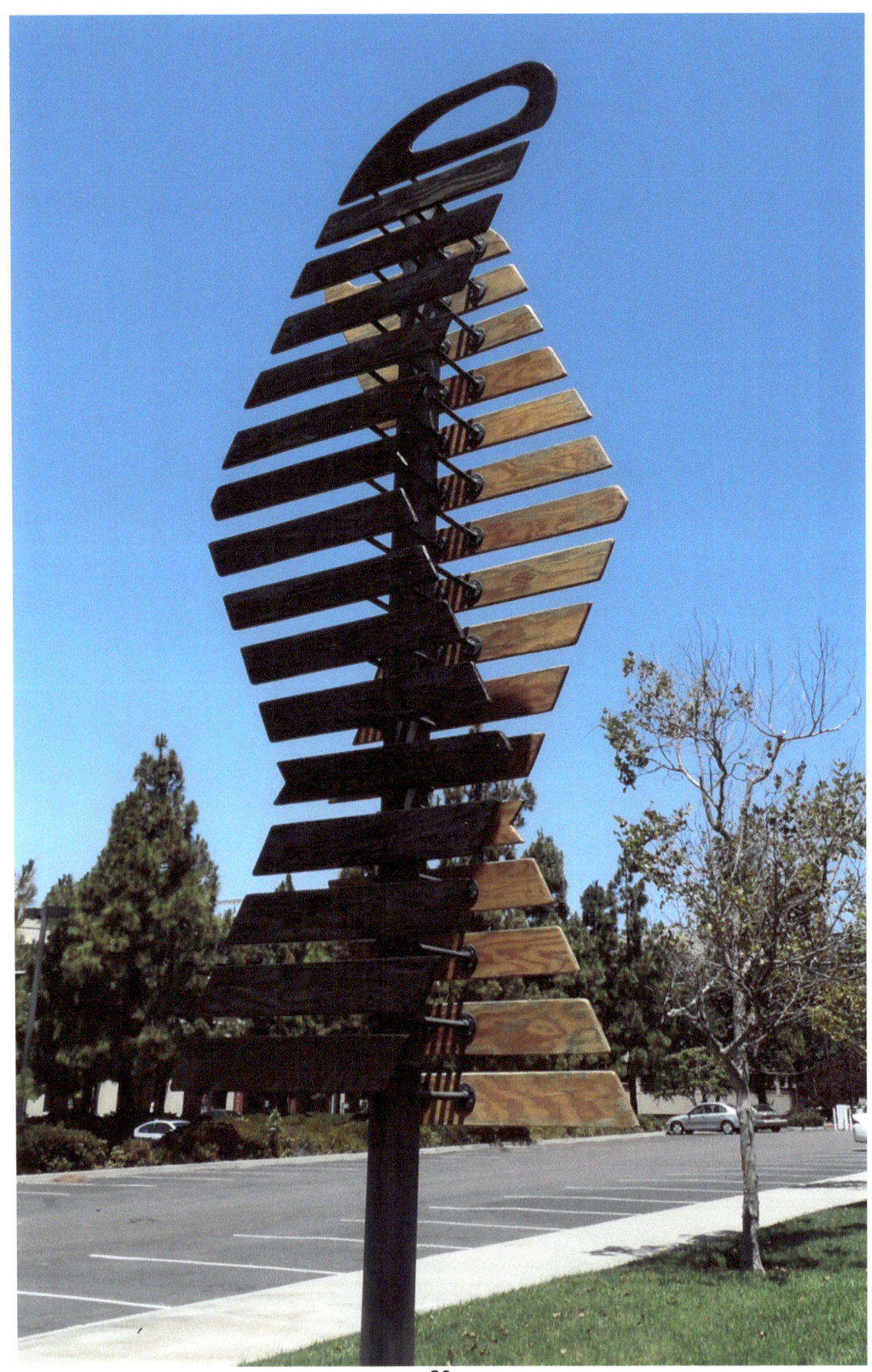

30
WAVE TREE by William Chris Brown

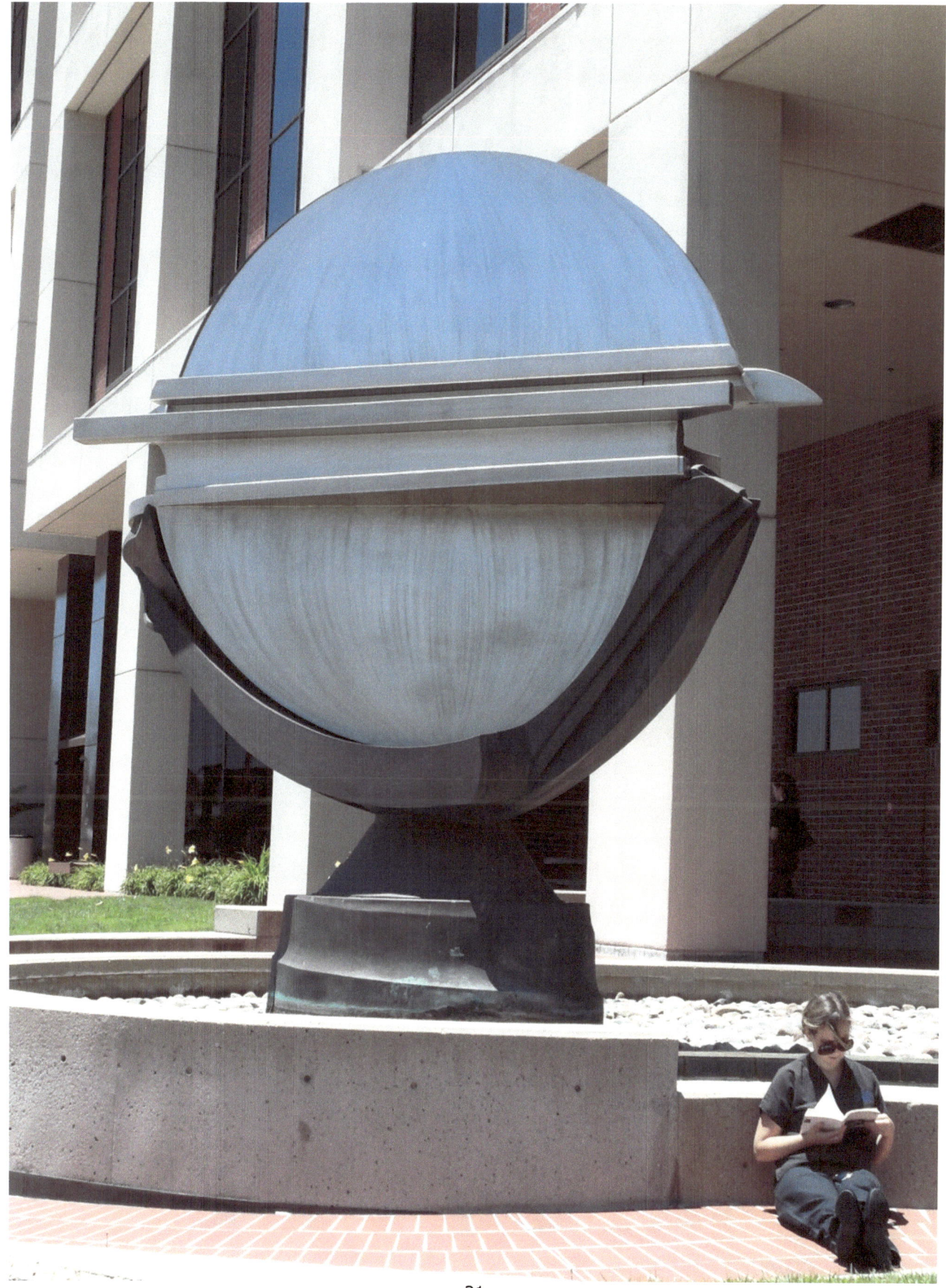

TRANSITION by Dan Dykes [donated by Scripps Foundation]

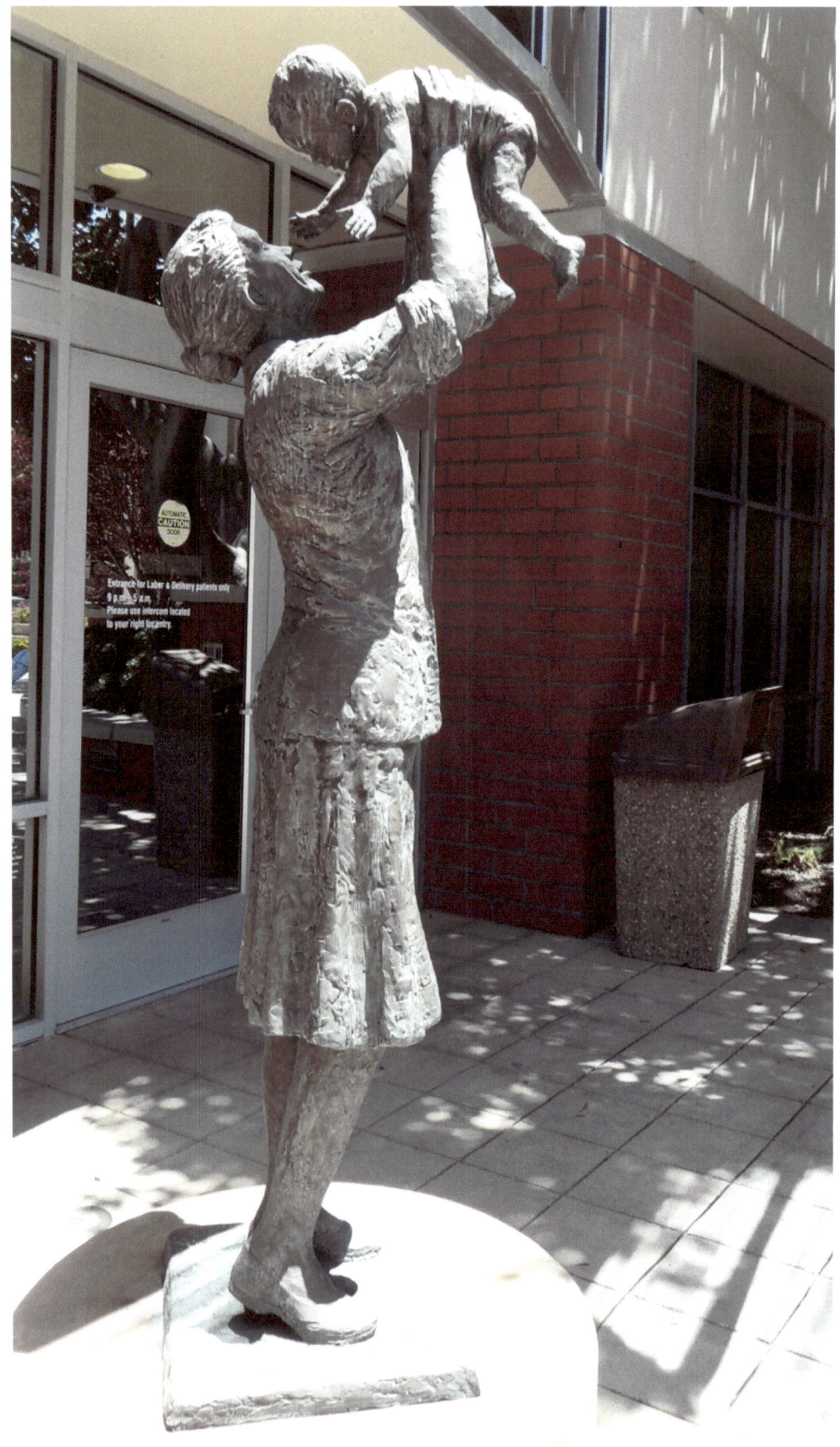

32
GRANDMA AND BABY by Dennis Smith [donated by Scripps Foundation]

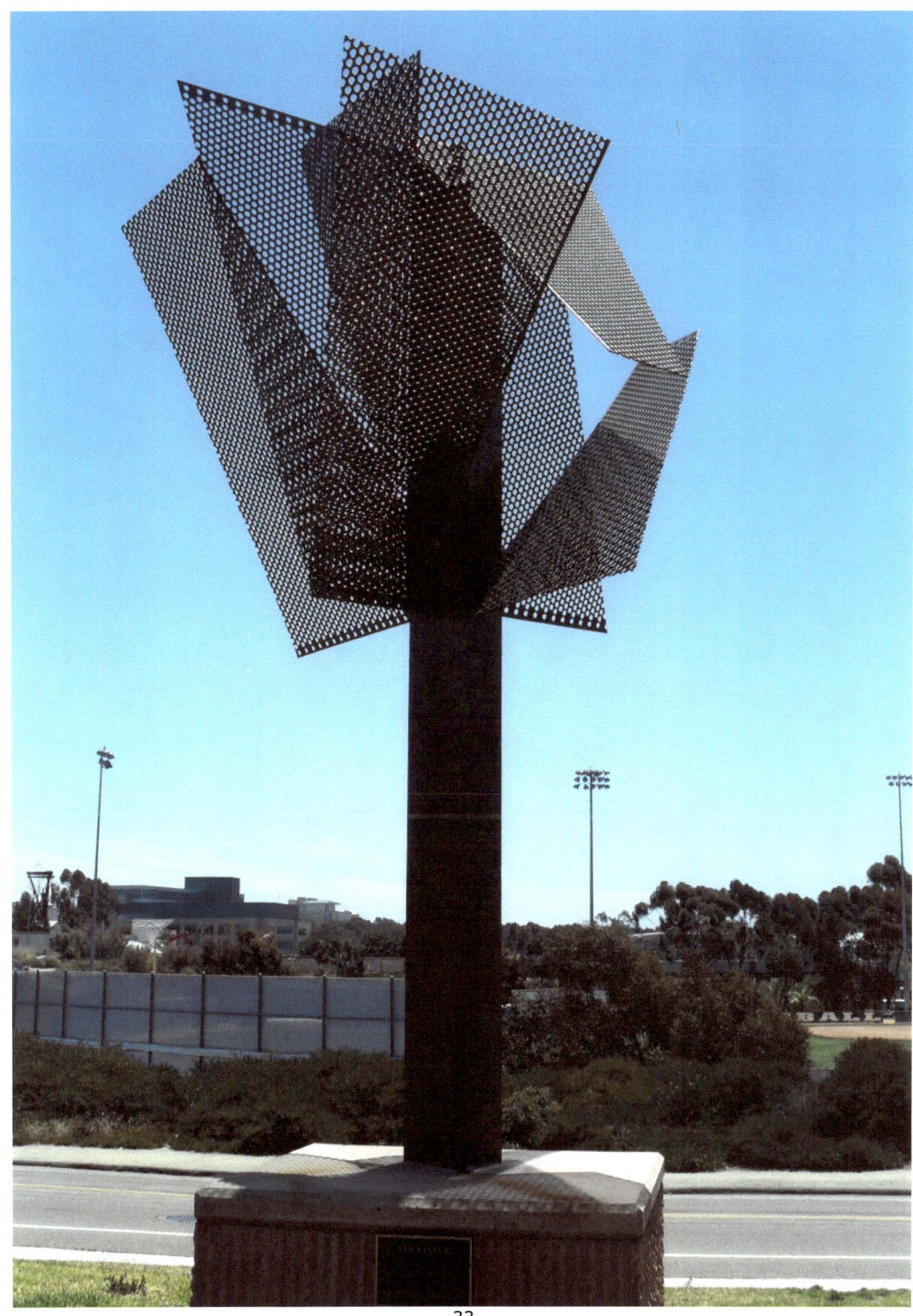

33

AIR FILTER by Viviana Lombrozo [donated by Viviana Lombrozo]

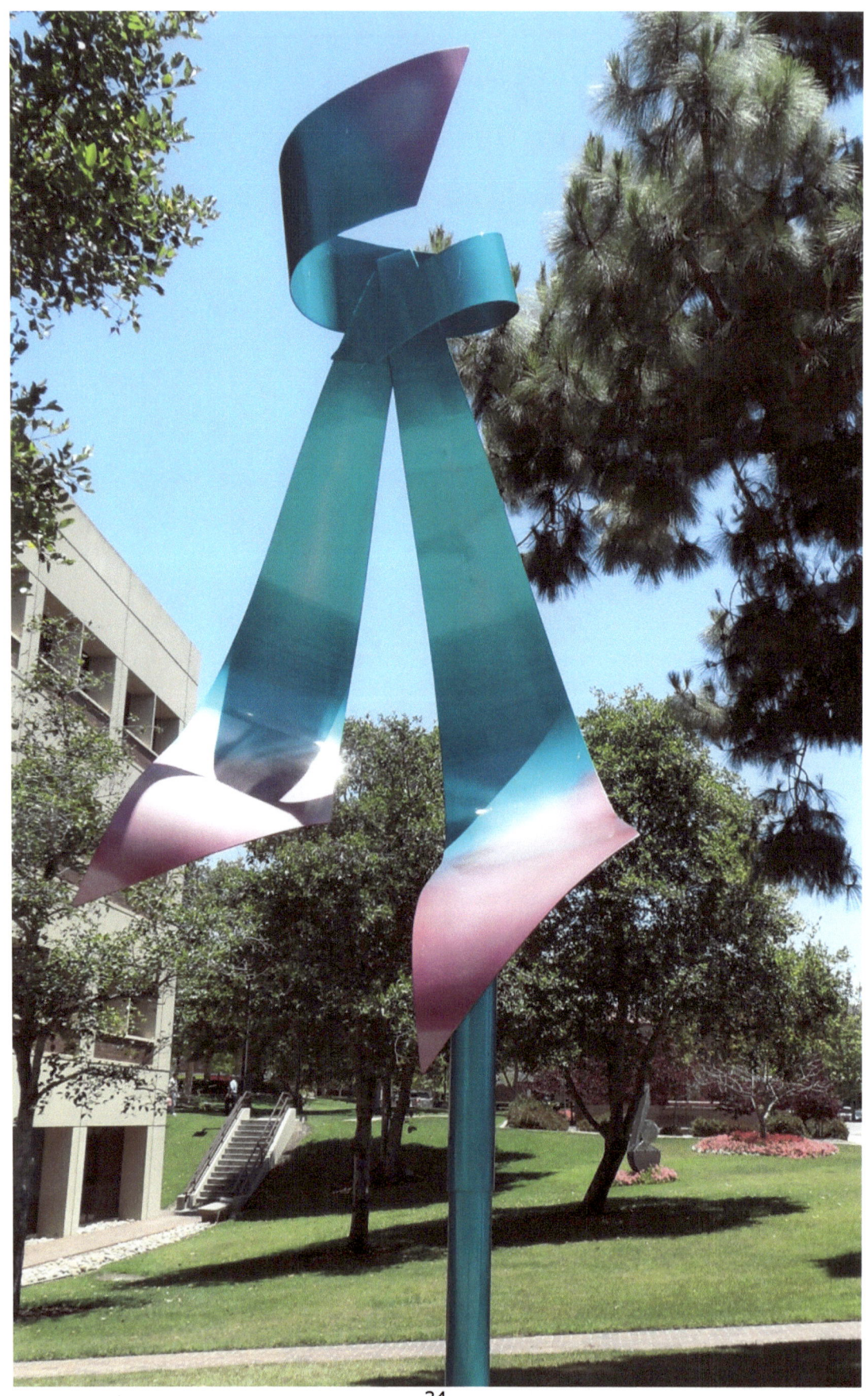

34
RIBBON OF HOPE by Lia Strell

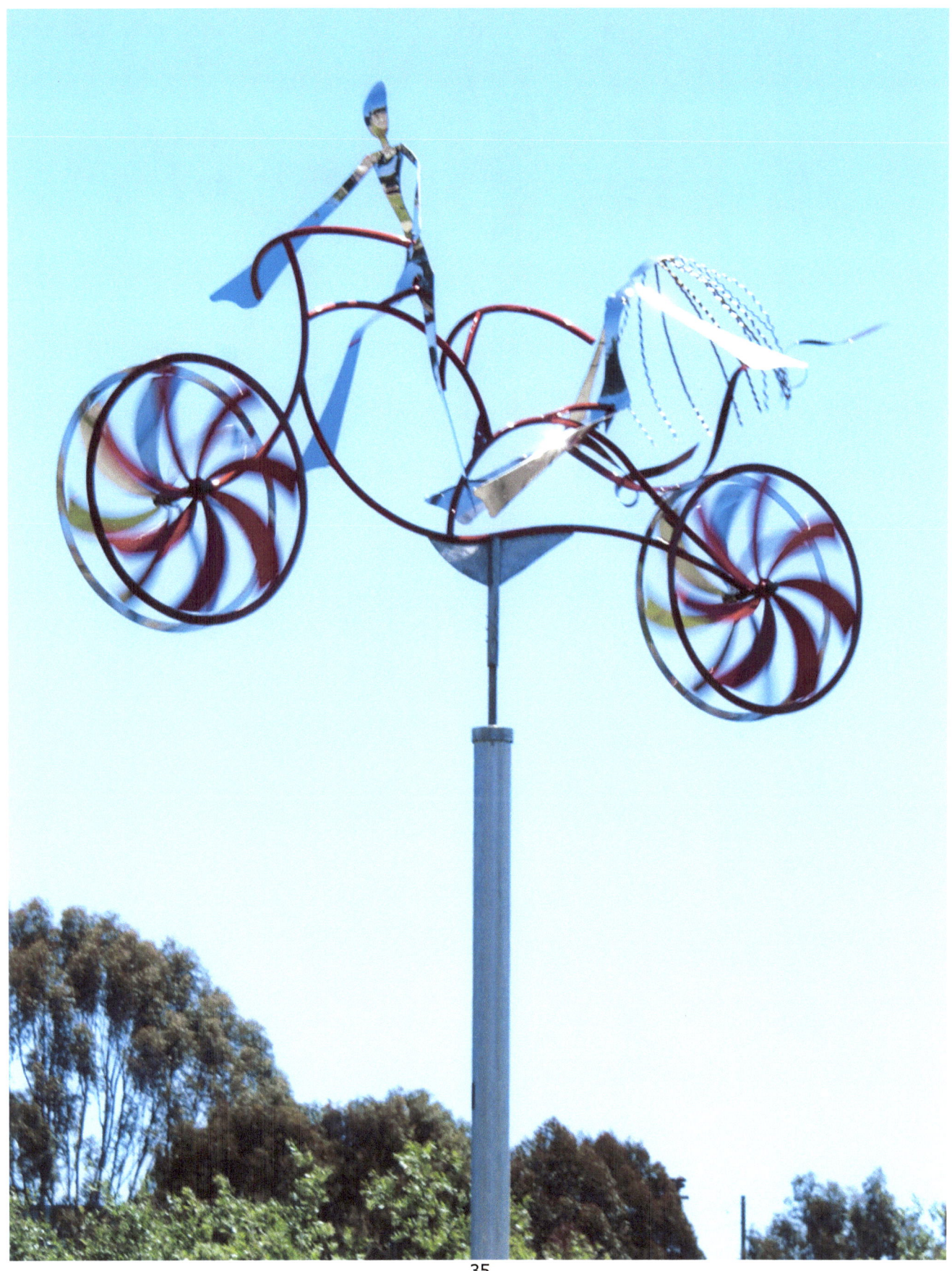

35
WE-E-E-E-E-E by Amos Robinson

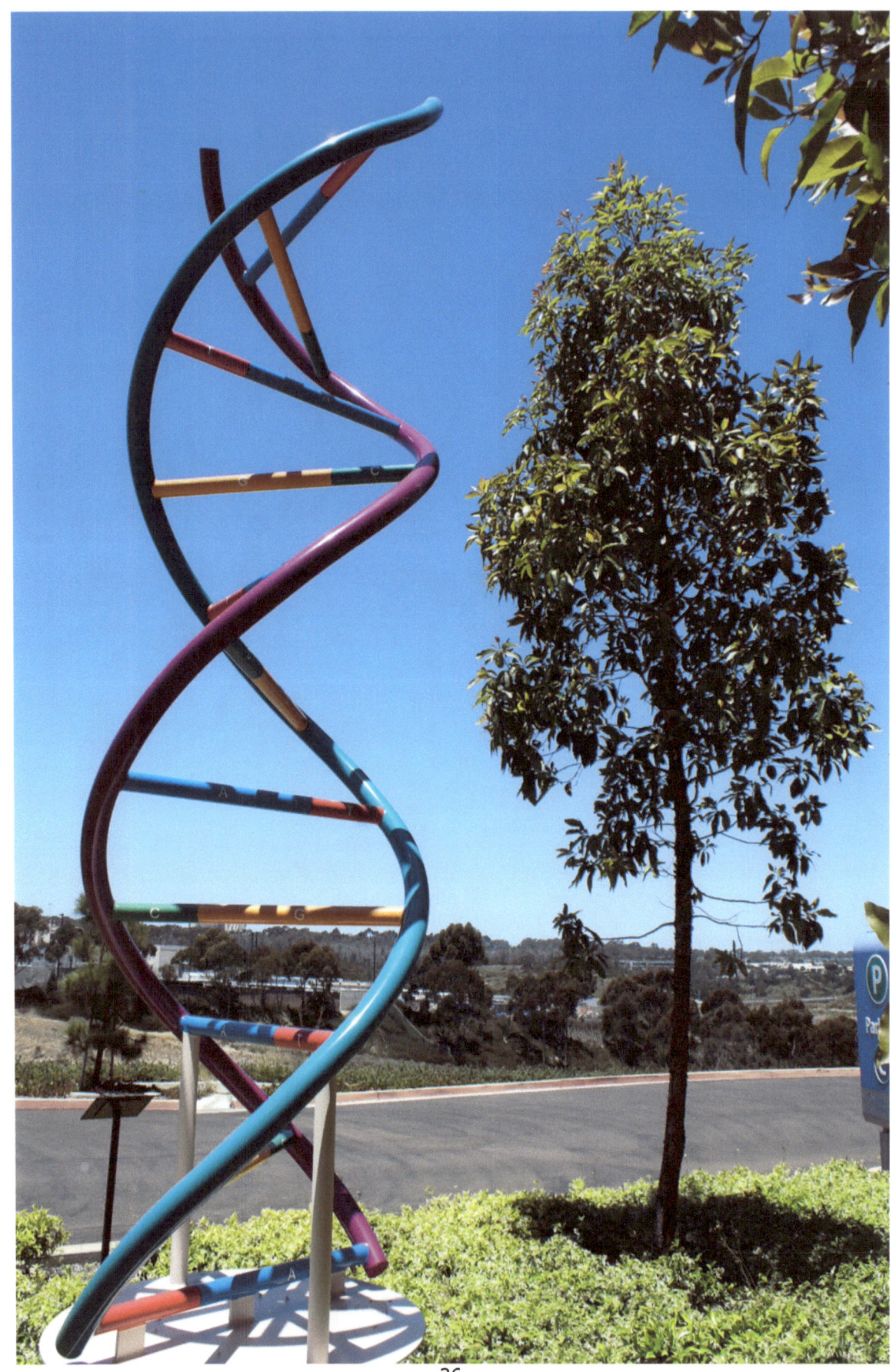

36
CHEMIS-TREE by Catherine Carlton

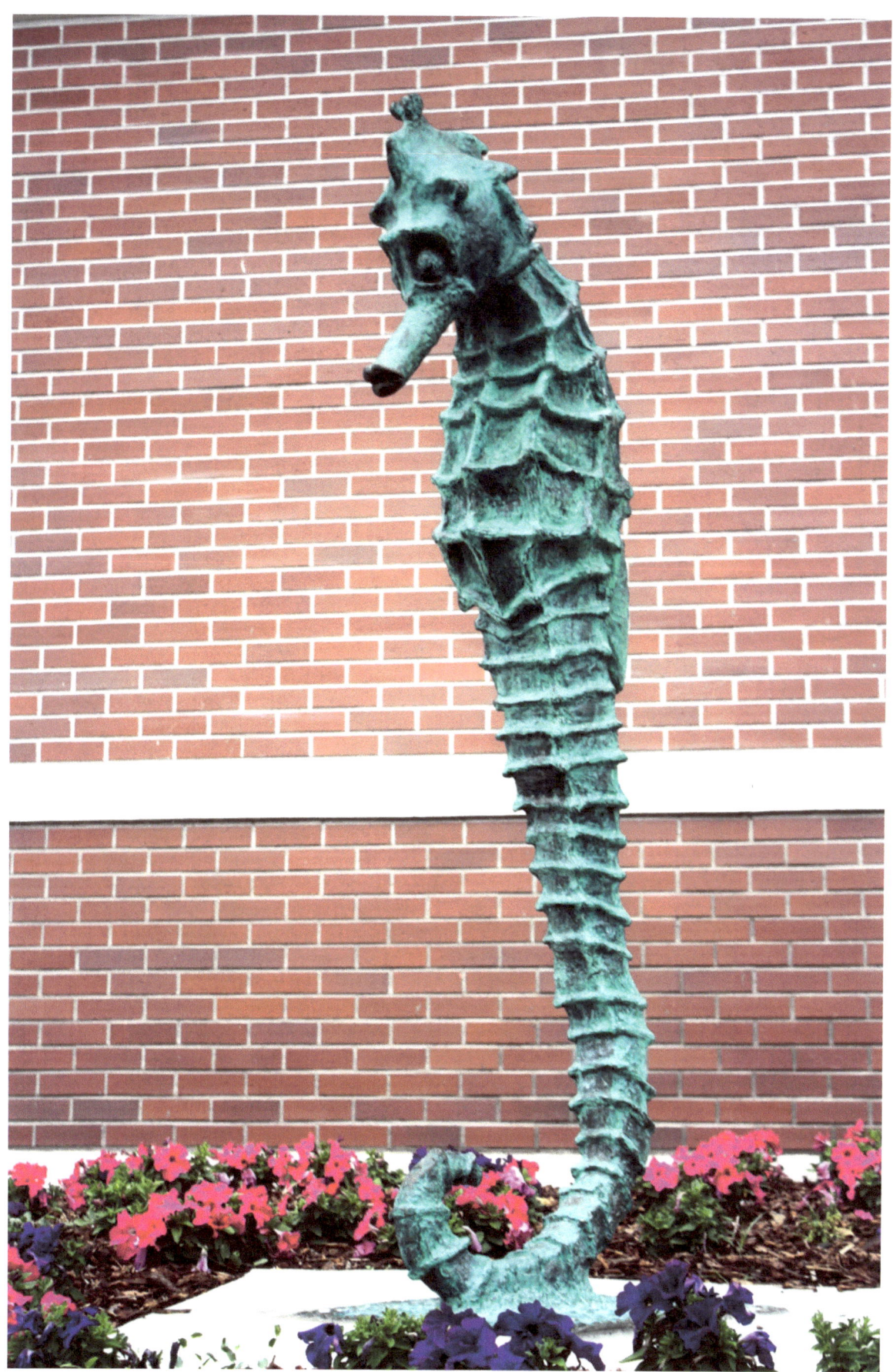

37
SEAHORSE by David "DJ" Brelje

Scripps Memorial Hospital Encinitas

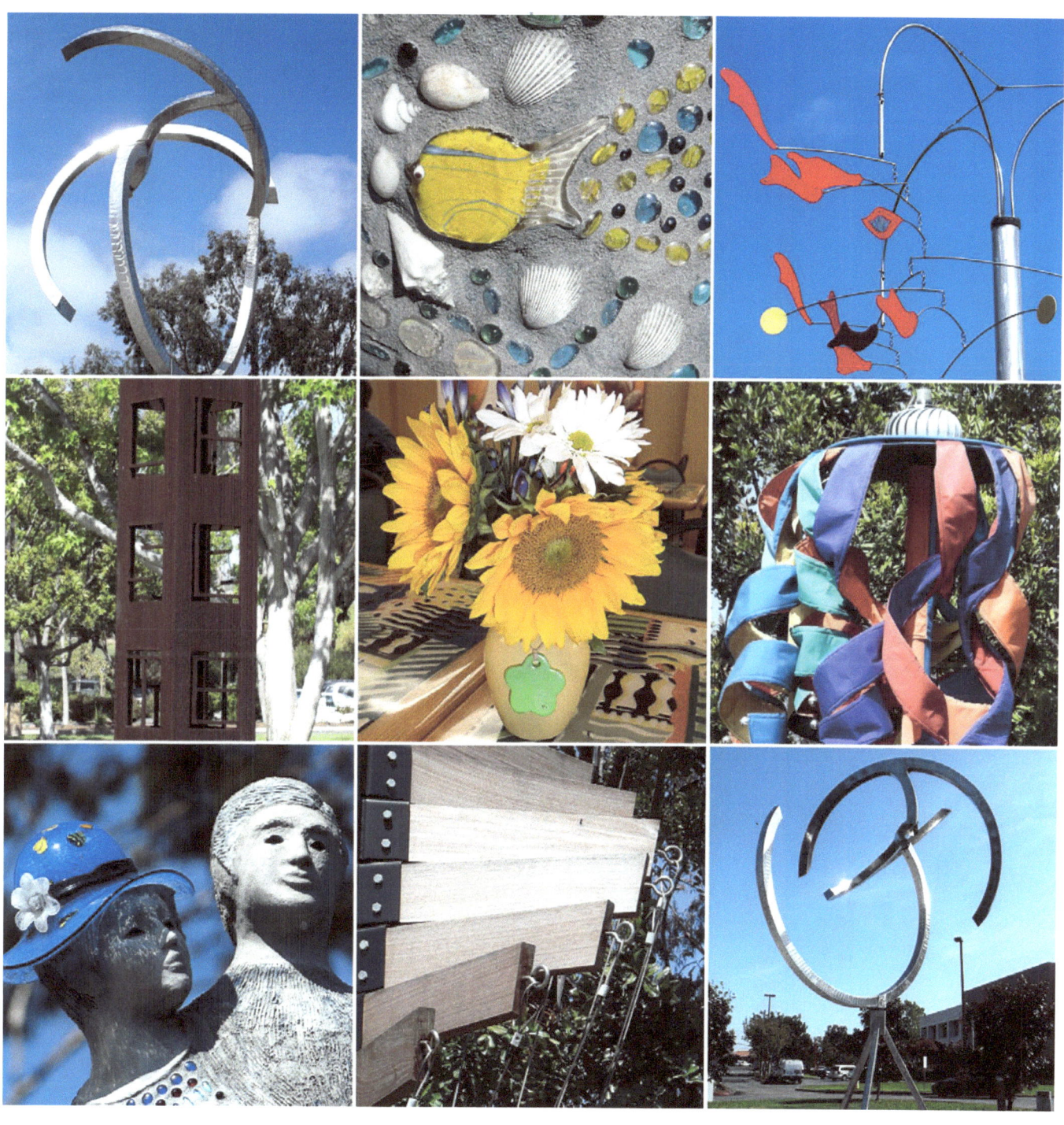

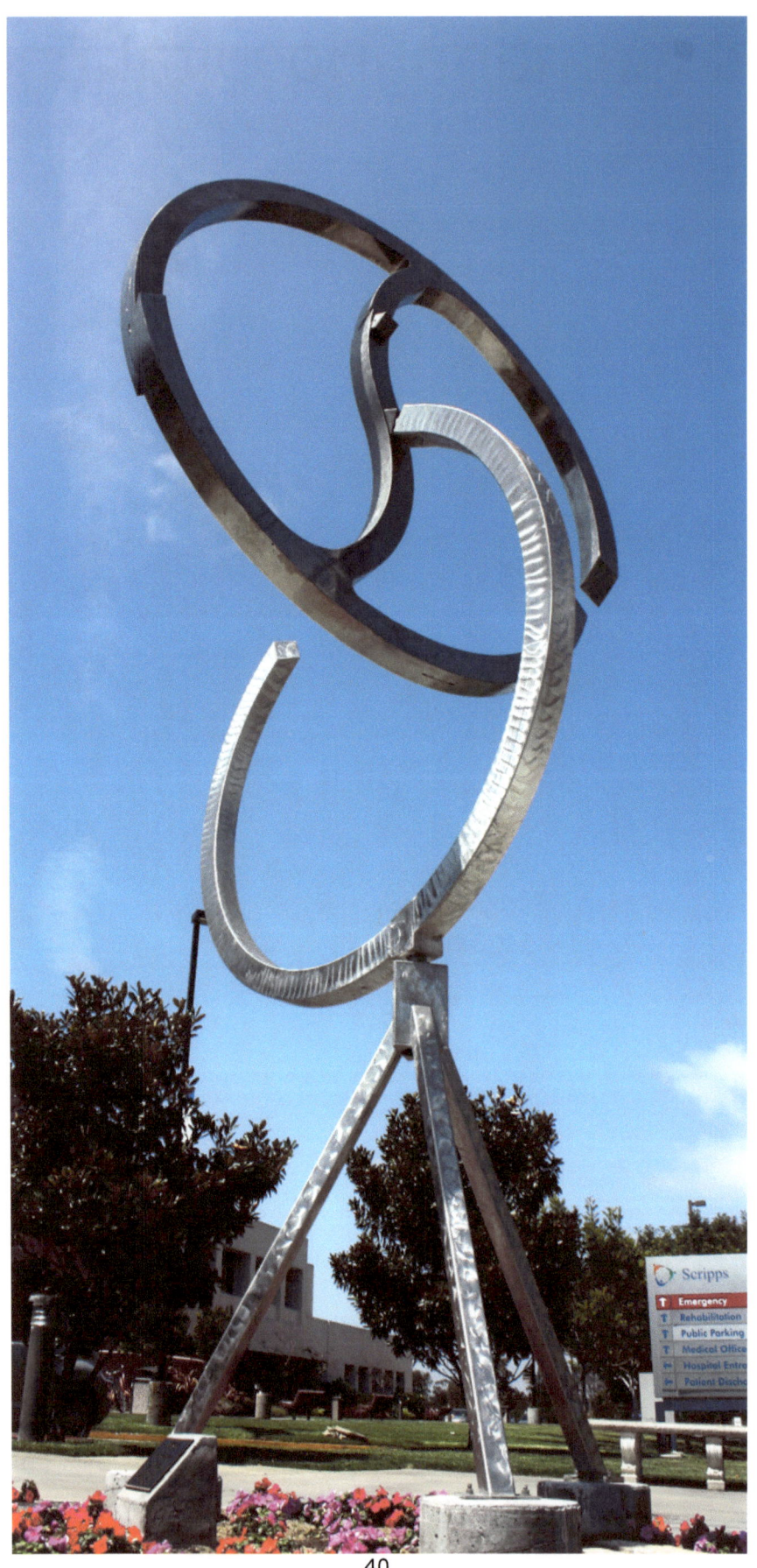

40

MIKOSHI by Jeffery Laudenslager

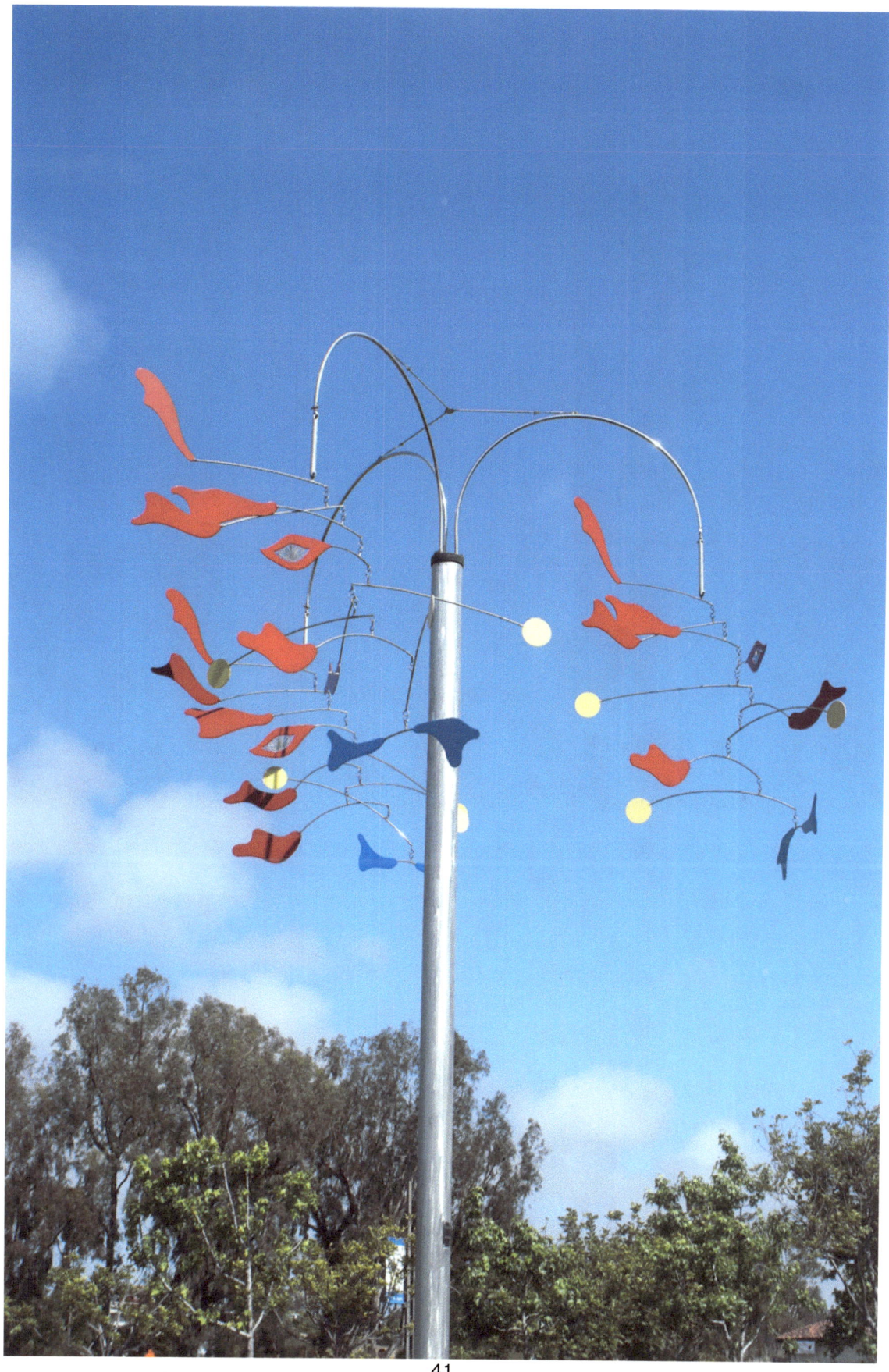

41
CALDERBERRY TREE by Amos Robinson

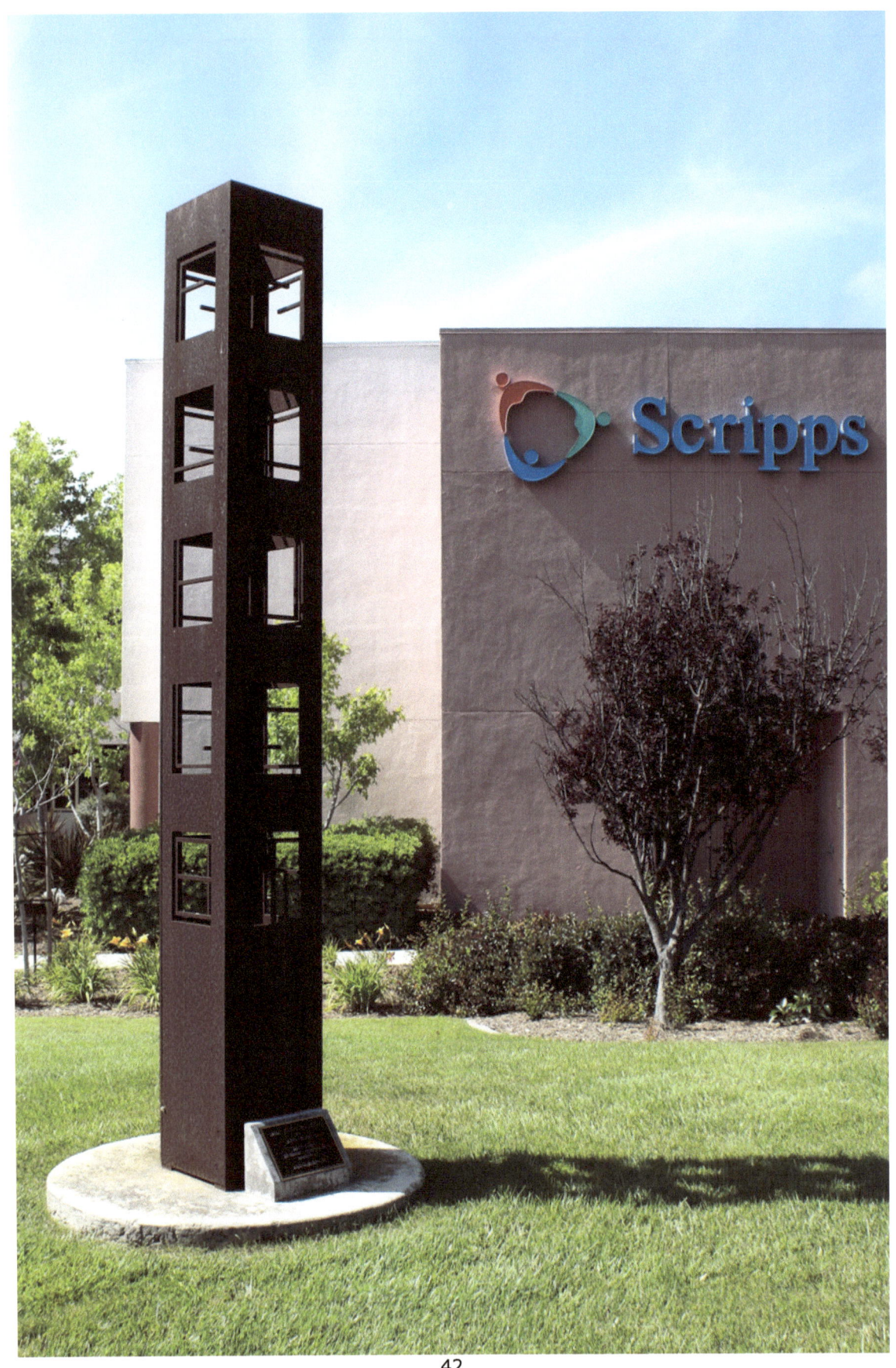

42
FAUST, FEAST, FABLE, FOLLY by Robin Bright

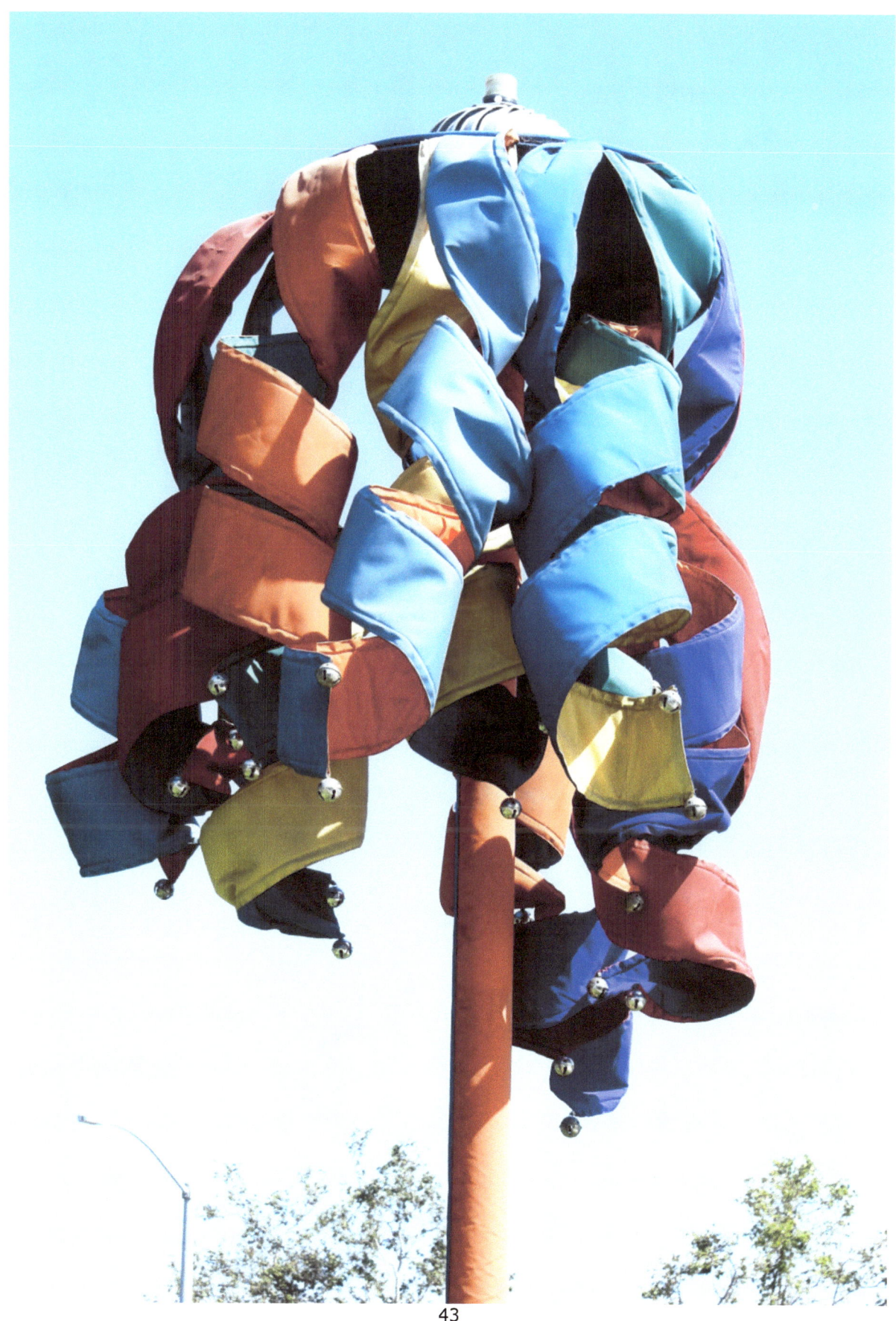

43
THE MAYPOLE TREE by Fritzie Urquhart

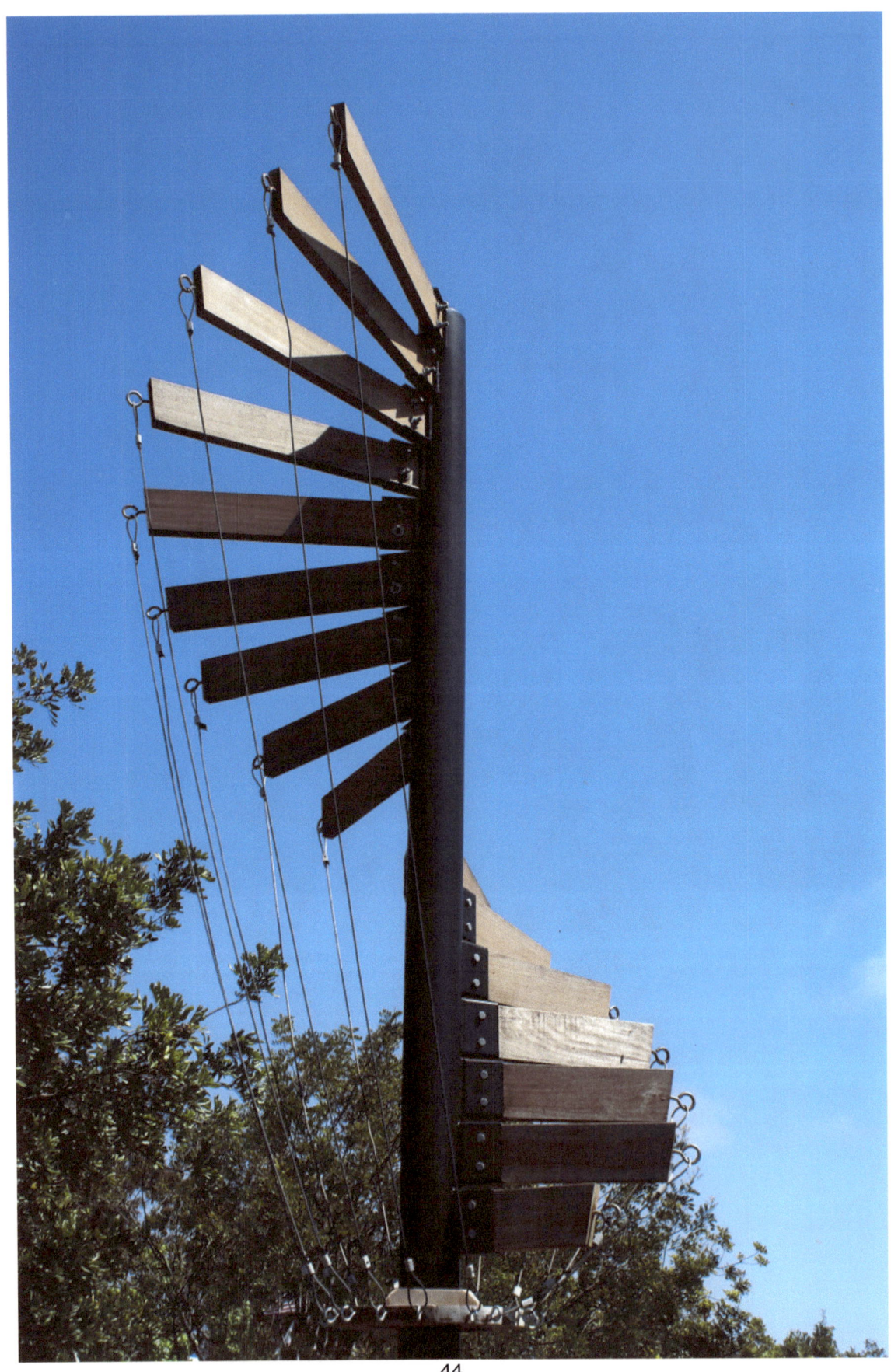

44
SPIRAL VOYAGE by Chris Brown

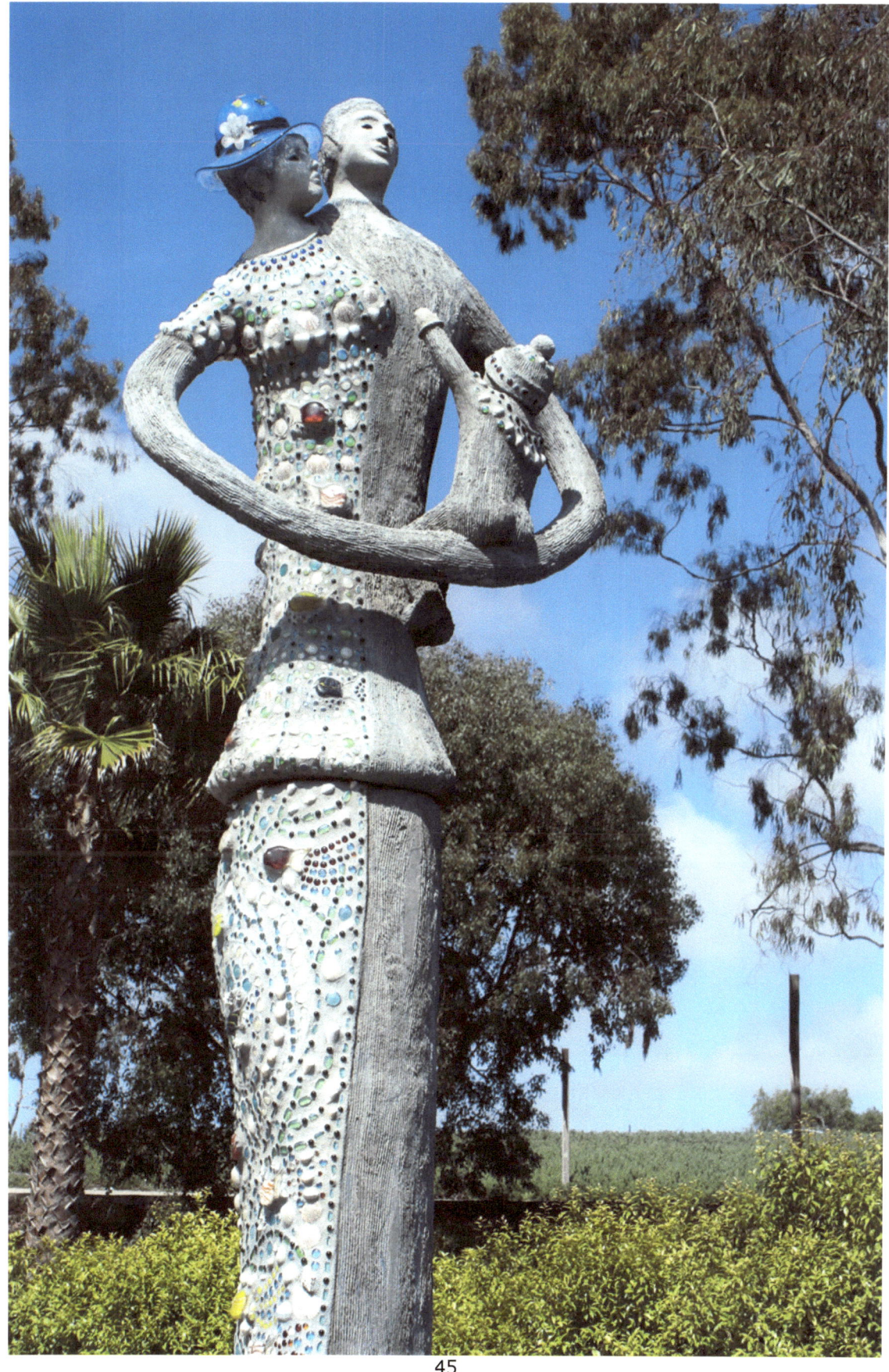

FAMILY TREE BY THE SEA by Carolyn Guerra [Gift to the Arts for Healing Program]

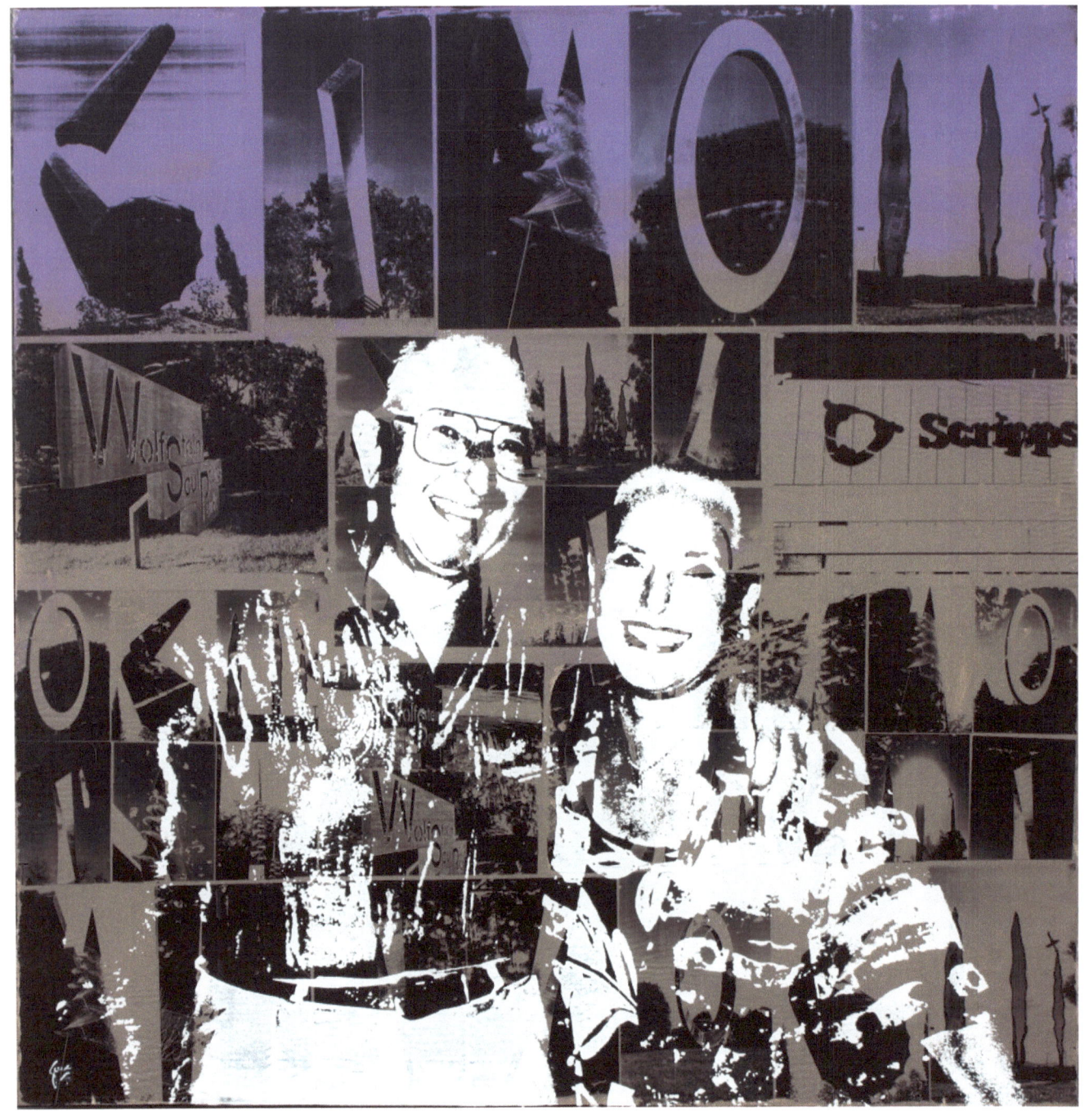

RALYN & NATHAN WOLFSTEIN

Our special thanks to the Scripps Health Foundation and the people at Scripps Memorial Hospitals, with their vision and enthusiasm this special "Arts for Healing" project has been made possible. We welcome all those who may choose to join us in this great endeavor.

For more information: **www.wolfsteinsculptureparks.com**